Options Help You to Generate Passive Income Guide for Beginners

Benefits of Options Trading and Volatility of the Options Market

Elijah Williams

Copyright 2022. All Rights Reserved.

This document provides exact and reliable information regarding the topic and issues covered. The publication is sold with the idea that the publisher is not required to render accounting, officially permitted, or otherwise qualified services. If advice is necessary, legal or professional, a practiced individual in the profession should be ordered.

From a Declaration of Principles which was accepted and approved equally by a Committee of the American Bar Association and a Committee of Publishers and Associations.

In no way is it legal to reproduce, duplicate, or transmit any part of this document in either electronic means or printed format. Recording of this publication is strictly prohibited, and any storage of this document is not allowed unless with written permission from the publisher. All rights reserved.

The information provided herein is stated to be truthful and consistent. Any liability, in terms of inattention or otherwise, by any usage or abuse of any policies, processes, or Instructions contained within is the solitary and utter responsibility of the recipient reader. Under no circumstances will any legal obligation or blame be held against the publisher for reparation, damages, or monetary loss due to the information herein, either directly or indirectly.

Respective authors own all copyrights not held by the publisher.

The information herein is offered for informational purposes solely and is universal as such. The presentation of the data is without a contract or any guarantee assurance.

TABLE OF CONTENTS

Introduction 5
Chapter 1. Guide for Beginners - Getting Started .. 27
Chapter 2. Tips and Tricks for Success 32
Chapter 3. How to Approach the Options Trading .. 41
Chapter 4. Rules for Successful Trading of Options 81
Chapter 5. Risk Management 94
Chapter 6. Designing a Trading Plan Flexibility: Adapting Your Strategy to Market Conditions 112
Chapter 7. Options Definition and Function 118
Chapter 8. Types of Options 121
Chapter 9. The Options Contract 129
Chapter 10. Options Trading 135
Chapter 11. The Volatility of the Options Market .. 145
Chapter 12. Benefits of Options Trading 148
Chapter 13. Options Help You to Generate Passive Income 152
Chapter 14. Options Provide Leverage for Your Investment 153
Conclusion 158

Introduction

An option is an agreement on the underlying shares of stock. It's an agreement to exchange shares at a fixed price over a specified timeframe (they can be bought or sold). The first thing that you should understand about options is the following. Why would someone get involved with the options trading in the first place? Most people come to options trading with the hope of earning profits from trading the options themselves. But to truly understand what you're doing, you need to understand why options exist, to begin with.

There are probably three main reasons that options on stocks exist. The first reason is that it allows people that have shares of stock to earn money from their investment in the form of regular income. So, it can be an alternative to dividend income or even enhance dividend income. As we are going to see you later, if you own a minimum of 100 shares of some stock, this is a possibility. Then you can sell options against the stock and earn income from that over time intervals lasting from a week to a month, generally speaking. Such a move entails some risk, but people will enter positions of that type when the relative risk is low.

The second reason that people get involved with options is that they offer insurance against a collapse of the stock. So, once again, an option involves being able to trade shares of the stock at a fixed price that is set at the time the contract is originated. One type of contract allows the buyer to purchase shares, the other allows the buyer to sell shares. This allows people who own large numbers of shares to purchase something that provides protection of their investment that would allow them to sell the shares at a fixed price, if their stock was declining by huge amounts on the market. So, the concept is exactly like paying insurance premiums. It's unclear how many people use this in practice, but this is one of the reasons that options exist. The way this would work would be that you pay someone a premium to secure the right to sell them your stock at a fixed price over some time frame. Then if the share price drops well below that degree to price, you would still be able to sell your shares and avoid huge losses that were occurring on the market.

The third reason that I would give for the

existence of options is that it provides a way for people to make arrangements to purchase shares of stock at the prices that they find attractive, which aren't necessarily available on the market. So, there is a degree of speculation here. But let's just say that a particular stock you are interested in is trading at $100 a share. Furthermore, let's assume that people are incredibly bullish on the stock and they are expecting it to rise by a great deal in the coming weeks. Maybe, it's earnings season.

During earnings season, stock can move by huge amounts. But before the earnings call, nobody knows whether the stock is going to go up or down or by how much it's going to move. An options contract could allow someone to speculate and set up a situation where they could profit from a huge move upward without having actually to invest in the stock.

So, in that situation, if the stock declined instead, they wouldn't be out of much money. Just for an example, let's say they buy an options contract that allows them to purchase the shares (of the stock currently at $100) for $102, and the option costs two dollars per share. So, the stock would have to go to

$104 or higher to make it worth it.

Typically, options contracts involve 100 shares. So, if the speculator bets wrong, the most they would be out would be $200.

Let's just say, after the earnings call, the share price jumps to $120. The speculator can exercise the option, which means they buy the shares at $102 per share. Then they can sell the stock on the market at the price of $120 per share. Taking into account the investment to buy the options contract, that leaves them with the sixteen $16 per-share profit. Now, you might say well why didn't they just buy the shares that $100 a share? The reason is if they did that, they would be exposed to the stock to the fullest extent possible. Like we said, earnings calls can go both ways. Just recently, Netflix announced that they lost subscribers. In after-hours trading alone, the stock lost $43 per share. So, in our little example, we could say that the stock dropped instead of gaining, let's say to $80 per share. In that case, our speculator would've been in a significant point of pain had they purchase the shares ahead of time. By doing the option instead, they set themselves up for profit while only risking a $200 loss. And it turns out that there are strategies you can use with options to profit no matter which way the stock moves. So, I didn't want to get too far ahead of we, but an experienced options trader would have set up a trade designed to earn profits either way.

Options Trading Basics - Advantages of Option Trading

Option trading has many advantages for investors. Essentially, it is an investment that offers an opportunity for those who have the capital to delve into an income generation venture. Advantages with options trading are multiple and should motivate people into the sector of trading securities, selling and buying assets as well as earning interests that accrue.

First is the ability of this venture to aid to manage risks when investing in stocks and securities. They can cushion one from having to incur losses in investment. This is because investing in the stocks and shares usually involves risks of all in the value of the shares. This devaluation can lead to a dwindling of the profits and may cut into the shares that one holds. However, the options marketing ensure that one is hedged from such uncertainty and as well as guarantees that a person can earn value from the trading of the shares.

Options trading is also advantageous is it allows someone the time to decide about purchase or not. This is particularly the advantage of the call options. The contract usually has a period during which a person considers the exercise of the implied rights. The person studies the market and its performance and has the allowance to understand his financial situation before deciding on whether to purchase the shares or not. This leads one to make decisions about investments that are reasoned out. It always comes with more preparedness to handle the consequences of the decisions that one takes. This helps to rid the habit of making trading decisions on whims that can later lead to anxiety and worry as market forces swing into play.

The freedom of action to exercise an option is also an exciting aspect of trading. This is because this is a speculative filed based on eth analysis of market forces and performance. Once one enters an option contract, they can happily enjoy trading them without the obligation to exercise the rights included in the contract. One can, in fact, just understand the market landscape and opt for a trade investment with an option that one does not even have intentions of exercising. On the speculative conception of options trading, one can decide just to exercise the purchase right in a call option when they know the market environment is getting better and promises value. They can also decide to exercise the sell option when losses are expected to avoid the loss or salvage a profit margin.

Leverage

Leverage is a very beneficial aspect of options trading that people try to take advantage of and participate in the security market. In leverage, one has to place smaller outlays with a prospect of making higher profits in view. This encourages those who do not have the capital to invest in the underlying assets or shares to find a way of investing and get returns. One of the essential parts of leverage is that one is usually getting back returns from the underlying assets or shares, yet they have not been required to pay the full cost for the purchase of the shares.

In the idea of leverage also is the advantage of diversification. This by creating a portfolio without incurring huge initial outlays. This diversification can then create a stream of investment channels that in practice, lead to profits increasing one's earnings. Sometimes this income can increase to go above one's dividends when one takes call options that are laid again the shares owned. This extra income can even emanate from the shares that are integrated having been acquired from a lending facility. Option premiums also come ahead of the trading activities and hence cushioning one from any chances of loss.

More On the Basics - How Options Work

After knowing the strategies and the reasons why to use options, let us now know how this type of trading works. Below are some of the details I have for you:

Options have a time frame. They always have their date of expiration. You should be able to know their time frame to make profits. After they expire, you do not have the right to purchase or offer stock for sale at a specified price. The shorter the time it has till expiry, the lower the value of the option.

Options have different strike prices, which generally indicate the price of the stock.

Options offer you the right to purchase or offer stock for sale.

Purchasing an option gives you the honor to purchase or offer the stock for sale.

Selling an option gives you the honor of delivering the stock at an agreed price. The stock's current price is not under consideration.

Types of Options

Market options have different types and categories. Standard types include calls and put options. Other options are classified based on securities, date of expiration, the styles they are using, and many others. We shall look at all the following categories.

Put option. It is an option contract where a trader holding this contract has the honor of offering the instrument for sale with an agreed future price. A trader purchases typically this option with the belief that the price of the asset will fall in the future.

Holders of put incur limited risks, unlike other options.

Call option. It is a contract that enables a trader to buy an instrument at an agreed future price. A trader purchases typically this option believing there will be an increment in asset price. Call options have their benefits, which include improved efficiency in the costs and reduced risks.

Exchange-traded options. It's a common options contract type. Any contract is an exchange-traded option if it is on the public traded exchange list. Any trader can exercise this type of option.

Over-the-counter option. Over the counter option is a complicated option contract. Usually happens in the over the counter market by private parties and not the general public making it less accessible.

Options based on the terms of the contracts are: American-style options. It isn't about the location. Options usually come with their date of expiration. American style option gives you the right to purchase or offer the asset for sale before any time of the date of expiration.

European-style option. This type of option is

different from the American style option. Here, the holder of the option contract possesses the right of purchasing or offering an asset for sale on the date of expiration and not any time before. This option is better than the American style option as it gives you some value.

Types of options based on the securities include the following:

Stock option. A stock option is an option type mostly based on the asset called shares in a public company.

Index option. An index option is quite like the stock option. It is mostly concerned with indexes and not assets. The holder of this option can purchase or offer indexes for sale at an agreed price before the date of expiration. Indexes in the market include Wilshire 5000, Nikkei 225, and many others.

Currency option. In this type of option, the holder of this contract has the right to purchase or offer any currency at a specific rate for sale.

Commodity option. Commodity option is a type of option that provides holders of the contract the honor to purchase and offer futures contracts for sale at a given strike price before the date of expiration.

Futures option. Futures option offers the owner the honor to purchase and offer a specific future contract for sale at a given price before the date of expiration.

Basket option. It is a type of option that offers the contract holder the honor of purchasing and offering for sale a group of market securities at a given price before the date of expiration. The group of securities may include stock, commodities, and even currencies.

Below is a list of the different types of options categorized according to the date of expiration:

Regular option. A regular option is a standard type of expiration cycle options. It gives the holder of this contract different months of the date of expiration. The months usually are four. You can select the month of expiration you want based on your preference.

Weekly option. A weekly option is quite like the regular option. It, however, gives the holder of this contract a shorter time for the date of expiration. It is also limited to some market securities and indices, unlike a regular option.

Quarterly option. This type of option is quite like a regular option. The difference is that quarterly options expire on the last day, unlike regular options, which expire on the last Friday of the month.

Long-term expiration option. As the name states, a long-term expiration option expires typically in January. It takes three years before it expires, unlike the other options in this category.

Other types of options include the following:

Employee stock option. Employee stock option is a type of option given to employees of either a public or a private company. It is given to employees as a bonus to compensate or retain them. The holders of this contract have the right to purchase some units of the capital of the company involved at an agreed price within a specific period.

Cash-settled option. A cash-settled option is applied when it is difficult to transfer an asset to the other party in the market. There is payment in cash of the profit made by a market participant of the contract to another one.

Exotic option. An exotic option is a customized option with sophisticated features, unlike other options. It takes place in the over the counter market. Some of the different types under this option include:

Barrier option. It is a type of exotic option that offers an amount to a holder of the contract when the price of the underlying instrument reaches or even surpasses the fixed one. Barrier options are less expensive and result in higher profits compared to other options. However, traders do not exercise them on the public, and due to the barrier features, they have maximum trade risks.

Binary option. It is a type of option which provides the holder of the contract a fixed amount in any cases of profit made before the date of expiration. These options have higher returns as compared to other traders. Binary options trading platforms are user-friendly for the less experienced traders to use.

Compound option. It is a type of exotic option that allows another option as its asset. Seen in the cases of a combination of calls and put options. Some of the benefits of compound options are that they are cheaper and have higher leverage as compared to other options.

Lookback option. It is an exotic option that

offers you the golden privilege of setting a market price by checking the prices of the asset and take advantage of the one with the most significant difference. A holder exercises this exotic option over the counter. The advantage of a lookback option is that it reduces risks in the market within the time given. However, this type of option is highly costly to execute in the market.

Chooser option. It is an exotic option that enables a contract holder to select either a put or a call when the date of expiration reaches. These options have similar strike prices and the date of expiration. Chooser options are of European style.

Trading Software and Operating Tools

First, there are generally two sites which are seen as the "best" for options trading: optionsXpress and TradeStation. Both of these have their perks and their reasons that you may decide to work through them.

OptionsXpress is a great place to start because they don't have an account minimum. They do ask a $12.95 commission on trades, and OptionsXpress only takes $1.25 for each contract.

The fees can be a tad iffy depending upon your trade volume but generally, the fees are low compared to other options. The other great thing about options trading by way of optionsXpress is that they have a lot of features that you'd really come expecting. For example, they offer real time quotes, and also allow you to look at options chains. Even better, optionsXpress doesn't charge you extra at all for using these tools. Bear in mind that in the world of finance, platforms will always favor those who are able to move more shares and who trade more often. But with that said, as far as a cost-effective options trading platform, OptionsXpress has you covered.

If you have a bit of money to invest, then you can go with TradeStation. TradeStation is generally ranked up there with optionsXpress in terms of powerful options trading platforms. And indeed, it's hard to find one much better than TradeStation. In exchange for a bit of a hefty account minimum, TradeStation offers you a vast number of useful tools tucked right into their super handy platform. For example, you'll find yourself using features like automatic trade execution rather often. TradeStation is also built for people who understand technology such that they can develop, test, and sell their own trading strategies to other enterprising investors who may have an interest in such a thing. Of course, this doesn't mean necessarily that you have to use this utility, but it can undoubtedly help you should you decide to use it. It has a high price tag with it, but it's complicated to find a platform that is much better than TradeStation at what it's supposed to do: be a simple and straightforward platform which is highly extensible and super easy to build upon, should that be what you're wanting.

However, these can get somewhat convoluted. What if you just wanted simple, low-cost, and easy to understand, then it's hard to beat eOption. eOption is fantastic for low-capital investors who want the platform to just simply get out of their way and let them do their own thing. eOptions has an account minimum of $500, which isn't too much in terms of options trading, and their rates are incredibly flat. They take a $3 trade commission, as well as fifteen cents for every contract that you decide to be involved with. If you haven't traded two times in the last year, or if you have less than ten thousand dollars in either your credit balances or your debit balances, you'll pay a fifty-dollar fee for "account inactivity". They have an incredibly low margin rate, which means that their trading costs are low. The only place that you might get caught up is that they have a lot of data fees and platform fees. These can be a veritable cash rainbow of prices, and clock in at anywhere from $1 to $200 in a month, or possibly even more depending upon what all you're doing on the platform. As far as design and ease of use, there's not too much that's different from the others; there are an array of features that are available to you. Nothing particularly stand-out or surprising, but it certainly isn't a drab platform either. It's well-featured and if you just want a simple and low-cost platform other than optionsXpress, it's incredibly challenging to find something that will fill those shoes better than eOptions.

  In terms of powerful trading platforms, there are two reigning kings: TD Ameritrade and OptionsHouse. Both have their own perks. Either one of these has one of the highest tech and fully loaded trading platforms that you can ask for, as well as with specifically useful features that you as the end user will find especially neat and handy.

TD Ameritrade doesn't have an account minimum and it takes a $9.99 trade commission. In addition, they have a promotion running which gives you six hundred dollars when you make a specified deposit. That can certainly be alluring in its own and give you a bit of extra capital to work with. TD Ameritrade operates on one of the most revered trading platforms in the business. Known as thinkorswim, this platform is specially created for active investors who are wanting the opportunity to get their hands on high quality tools and research, as well as who would like to try out different strategies or practice cost observation by analyzing the risks and benefits of specific interactions they could make on the marketplace. In addition, TD Ameritrade offers the Trade Architect service, based on the internet, as well as a Mobile Trader application for smartphones and other mobile devices. Should one use Trade Architect instead of thinkorswim, they'll find it lacking a bit in tools and services compared to the awe-inspiring thinkorswim, but nevertheless they'll still find an absolute wealth of sophisticated features that they'll find useful regardless.

The other super impressive platform that one

may be interested in is aligned with the OptionsHouse eTrade broker. They offer a vast array of tools which are usually relegated to financial professionals who make an entire career out of carefully watching and analyzing the markets in different ways. In other words, they have a vast number of tools that will benefit the type who wants to be an active trader. OptionsHouse too has a decent trade commission: $4.95 per trade. They don't have a specific account minimum, and they offer a thousand dollars in free commissions when you make a specified deposit.

Lastly, there are a couple platforms which offer a significant amount of utility in another way: the absolute wealth of market research and market data that they'll have available for free to any enterprising users who decide to use these services. In this category are Charles Schwab and Fidelity.

Fidelity has a $7.95 trade commission and a $2,500 account minimum. However, in return for this hefty minimum and hefty commission rate, you get access to one of the best stores of knowledge in the industry. They get a considerable amount of research, more significant than almost anybody else, and they offer a lot of research from over twenty industry giants, such as McLean Capital Management. They make it super easy to access all of this and it also comes free with your account. They also offer an application for your mobile device which lets you access all of the research by way of your phone's built-in web browser. If you're looking for raw research, it's hard to do any better than using Fidelity Investments as your broker.

However, there is a tad more to knowledge than simply research, and Charles Schwab excels where Fidelity falls short. They have a $6.95 trade commission and a $1,000 account minimum. Additionally, they'll give you five hundred dollars in cash if you make a specified deposit, which once again could be useful for building up some expendable capital to use for your trading. In addition to a lot of raw research, Schwab has a tremendous amount of support for active traders, offering things such as trade assessment tools to allow you to see whether or not a trade you'd like to make is a bright idea. However, they also offer to you a ton of options market discourse by the analysts hired by Schwab, as well as seminars, both live and pre-recorded, both online and in-person. What's more is that the in-person seminars are free to users of the service, because Schwab has a lot of branches throughout the country. What's more is that Schwab offers two top-notch platforms for stock trading. One is geared towards newer options traders, called StreetSmart, and the other is geared towards far more active traders, called StreetSmart Edge.

Really, knowing what options broker to go with is a matter of knowing yourself and your situation. Do you have a lot to spend on options trading? If you don't have a lot of investment capital, it's much better to start small and not invest too much in the first place, since your capital matters more to you by virtue of there being less of it. If you have a lot of investment capital and a basic idea of how to trade options, you'd be served well to go with one of the more research-heavy brokers geared at active traders. That too is a consideration in and of itself; do you want trading to be a significant part of your life? For example, do you want to do more with trading than just check the market every morning before work and night before bed? Do you want to spend a significant amount of time working on your portfolio and evaluating specific decisions to see which one would result in you making the most significant profit? If so, then you might find that you'd find yourself happier in the ones with a greater wealth of tools.

Chapter 1. Guide for Beginners - Getting Started

Walking you through the learning curve of options trading will always start with the most basic move you'll need to make setting yourself up in a position actually to be able to trade.

To do that, you're going to need an options account.

One thing to know before you pick your firm: times have changed considerably over the last couple of decades when it comes to options trading. Back before the internet became such a constant part of our lives, your brokerage firm – or, at least, your personal representative at the firm – would make your options trades on your behalf and you paid a hefty price for their services. Nowadays, however, you'll be doing most of your trades yourself.

Commission for your representative is thus a whole lot lower than it used to be, which means it won't cost you an arm and both legs to rely on your rep in the early days of your experience. While you are learning, feel free to make use of your firm's services to place and confirm your trades, if it helps you feel more comfortable getting to know the process.

With this in mind, there are going to be certain things to look for when you select your firm:

Compare commission prices to make sure you're getting a great deal.

Make sure the firm has up to date software and is capable of setting up trades quickly and reliably to make sure you get those trades you want at the best prices.

Check out the hours of service to ensure they are compatible with your needs. In these days of online firms, you could be dealing with a firm that's across the ocean from the markets you have an interest in, or you might find that a firm only makes its reps available for the length of the working day, which might not suit your own timing.

Speak personally with the reps at the firm, as these are the people who are going to help you during the process of setting up your strategy. You want someone who is personable and knowledgeable – and, most importantly, who speaks in terms that you personally find easy to comprehend.

Take a look at the additional services the firm supplies. Many will offer learning materials, guides and even classes or webinars to help you hone your strategies. Even if you feel that you know all you need to know already, there's no harm in a refresher course or a little nugget of inspiration every once in a while.

Once you select a firm, you'll then need to consider signing a "margin agreement" with that firm. This agreement allows you to borrow money from the firm in order to purchase your stocks, which is known as "buying on margin".

Understandably, your brokerage firm is not going to allow you to do that if you don't have the financial status to pay them back. They will therefore run a credit check on you and ask you for information about your resources and knowledge.

A margin account is not a necessity for options

trading – you don't actually use margin to purchase an option, because it must be paid for in full. However, it can be useful as you graduate to more advanced strategies – in some cases, it will be obligatory. If you opt to sign a margin agreement, talk it through thoroughly with the firm as there are certain restrictions on the type of money you can use that may apply to you.

Next, you'll need to sign an "options agreement" – and, this time, it's an obligatory step. This agreement is designed to find out how much you know about options and how much experience you have of trading them. It also aims to ensure that you are absolutely aware of the risks you take by trading and make sure that you are financially able to handle those risks.

By ascertaining these things, your firm can determine what level of options trading you should be aiming for. It will therefore approve your "trading level", of which there are five:

Level 1: You may sell covered calls

Level 2: You may buy calls and puts and also buy strangles, straddles and collars. You may also sell puts that are covered by cash and by options on exchange-traded funds and indexes

Level 3: You may utilize credit and debit spreads

Level 4: You may sell "naked puts", straddles and strangles

Level 5: You may sell "naked indexes" and "index spreads"

For now, all you need to be aware of is that your firm will determine for you which level you should be at. As a beginner, don't be surprised if you only reach the first two levels.

Once you've signed the agreement, you'll be handed a booklet that contains a mine of information about risks and rewards within options trading. Right now, if you were to read that booklet, it would seem to be in a foreign language. By the time you finish this crash course, it will be a lot more decipherable – and it's very important for your success that you do read it.

Finally, your firm will present you with a "standardized option contract". It's the same for every trader, which means you stand the same chance of success as every other person out there in the options market.

By trading an option, you are entering into a legal agreement that is insured by the Options Clearing Corporation, which guarantees the contract will be honored in full. Make sure you read that contract to be aware of not only the rights you have as a trader, but also the obligations you must follow in the same role.

Congratulations, you have an options account. This is the conduit through which you will create and implement your strategies and begin your adventure in options trading.

Chapter 2. Tips and Tricks for Success

Know when to go off book: While sticking to your plan, even when your emotions are telling you to ignore it, is the mark of a successful trader, this in no way means that you must blindly follow your plan 100 percent of the time. You will, without a doubt, find yourself in a situation from time to time where your plan is going to be rendered completely useless by something outside of your control. You need to be aware enough of your plan's weaknesses, as well as changing market conditions, to know when following your predetermined course of action is going to lead to failure instead of success. Knowing when the situation really is changing, versus when your emotions are trying to hold sway is something that will come with practice, but even being aware of the disparity is a huge step in the right direction.

Avoid trades that are out of the money: While there are a few strategies out there that make it a point of picking up options that are currently out of the money, you can rest assured that they are most certainly the exception, not the rule. Remember, the options market is not like the traditional stock market which means that even if you are trading options based on underlying stocks buying low and selling high is just not a viable strategy. If a call has dropped out of the money, there is generally less than a 10 percent chance that it will return to acceptable levels before it expires which means that if you purchase these types of options what you are doing is little better than gambling, and you can find ways to gamble with odds in your favor of much higher than 10 percent.

Avoid hanging on too tightly to your starter strategy: Your core trading strategy is one that should always be constantly evolving as the circumstances surrounding your trading habits change and evolve as well. What's more, outside of your primary strategy you are going to want to eventually create additional plans that are more specifically tailored to various market states or specific strategies that are only useful in a narrow band of situations. Remember, the more prepared you are prior to starting a day's worth of trading, the greater your overall profit level is likely to be, it is as simple as that.

Utilize the spread: If you are not entirely risk averse, then when it comes to taking advantage of volatile trades the best thing to do is utilize a spread as a way of both safeguarding your existing investments and, at the same time, making a profit. To utilize a long spread, you are going to want to generate a call and a put, both with the same underlying asset, expiration details, and share amounts but with two very different strike prices. The call will need to have a higher strike price and will mark the upper limit of your profits and the put will have a lower strike price that will mark the lower limit of your losses. When creating a spread, it is important that you purchase both halves at the same time as doing it in fits and spurts can add extraneous variables to the formula that are difficult to adjust for properly.

Never proceed without knowing the mood of the market: While using a personalized trading plan is always the right choice, having one doesn't change the fact that it is extremely important to consider the mood of the market before moving forward with the day's trades. First and foremost, it is important to keep in mind that the collective will of all of the traders who are currently participating in the market is just as much as a force as anything that is more concrete, including market news. In fact, even if companies release good news to various outlets and the news is not quite as good as everyone was anticipating it to be then related prices can still decrease.

Never get started without a clear plan for entry and exit: While finding your first set of entry/exit points can be difficult without experience to guide you, it is extremely important that you have them locked down prior to starting trading, even if the stakes are relatively low. Unless you are extremely lucky, starting without a clear idea of the playing field is going to do little but lose your money. If you aren't sure about what limits you should set, start with a generalized pair of points and work to fine tune it from there.

More important than setting entry and exit points, however, is using them, even when there is still the appearance of money on the table. One of the biggest hurdles that new options traders need to get over is the idea that you need to wring every last cent out of each and every successful trade. The fact of the matter is that, as long as you have a profitable trading plan, then there will always be more profitable trades in the future which means that instead of worrying about a small extra profit you should be more concerned with protecting the profit that the trade has already netted you. While you may occasionally make some extra profit ignoring this advice, odds are you will lose far more than you gain as profits peak unexpectedly and begin dropping again before you can effectively pull the trigger.

Never double down: When they are caught up in the heat of the moment, many new options traders will find themselves in a scenario where the best way to recoup a serious loss is to double down on the underlying stock in question at its newest, significantly lowered, price in an effort to make a profit under the assumption that things are going to turn around and then continue to do so to the point that everything is completely profitable once again. While it can be difficult to let an underlying stock that was once extremely profitable go, doubling down is rarely if ever going to be the correct decision. If you find yourself in a spot where you don't know if the trade you are about to make is actually going to be a good choice, all you need to do is ask yourself if you would make the same one if you were going into the situation blind, the answer should tell you all you need to know.

Never take anything personally: It is human nature to build stories around, and therefore form relationships with, all manner of inanimate objects including individual stocks or currency pairs. This is why it is perfectly natural to feel a closer connection to particular trades, and possibly even consider throwing out your plan when one of them takes an unexpected dive. Thinking about and acting on are two very different things, however, which is why being aware of these tendencies are so important to avoid them at all costs.

This scenario happens just as frequently with trades moving in positive directions as it does negative, but the results are always going to be the same. Specifically, it can be extremely tempting to hang on to a given trade much longer than you might otherwise decide to simply because it is on a hot streak that shows no sign of stopping. In these instances, the better choice of action is to sell off half of your shares instead and then set a new target based on the updated information to ensure you are in a position to have your cake and eat it too.

Not taking your choice of broker seriously: With so many things to consider, it is easy to understand why many new option traders simply settle on the first broker that they find and go about their business from there. The fact of the matter is, however, that the broker you choose is going to be a huge part of your overall trading experience which means that the importance of choosing the right one should not be discounted if you are hoping for the best experience possible. This means that the first thing that you are going to want to do is to dig past the friendly exterior of their website and get to the meat and potatoes of what it is they truly offer. Remember, creating an eye-catching website is easy, filling it will legitimate information when you have ill intent is much more difficult.

Find a Mentor: When you are looking to go from causal trader to someone who trades successfully on the regular, there is only so much you can learn by yourself before you need a truly objective eye to ensure you are proceeding appropriately. This person can either be someone you know in real life, or it can take the form of one or more people online. The point is you need to find another person or two who you can bounce ideas off of and whose experience you can benefit from. Options trading doesn't need to be a solitary activity; take advantage of any community you can find.

Knowledge is the key: Without some type of information which you can use to assess your trades, you are basically playing at the roulette table. Even poker players show up to the table with a game plan. They can adapt to the circumstances and learn to read other players. That way, they can tell the contenders from the pretenders. Options trading is no different. If you are unable to use the information that is out there to your advantage, then what you will end up with is a series of guesses which may or may not play out. Based purely on the law of averages you have a 50/50 chance of making money. That may not seem like bad odds, but a string of poor decisions will leave you in the poor house in no time.

So, it is crucial that you become familiar with the various analytics and tools out there which you can use to your advantage. Bear in mind that everyone is going to be looking at the same information. However, it is up to you to figure out what can, or might, happen before everyone else does. This implies really learning and studying the numbers so that you can detect patterns and see where trends are headed, or where trends may reverse. The perfect antidote to that is vision and foresight. Practice building scenarios. Try to imagine what could happen is trends continue. Or, what would happen if trends reversed? What needs to happen in order for those trends to continue or reverse?

Chapter 3. How to Approach the Options Trading

How Do You Start Investing in the Stock Market

The first step to start investing in the stock market is to know what the stock exchange is. It might seem obvious, but it's not like that: many traders start stock trading without even knowing what it is. The Stock Exchange is the regulated financial market on which shares are exchanged, which represent securities owned by listed companies. Each share gives the right, as the case may be, to receive a dividend (a portion of the company profits that are redistributed) and to participate in the ordinary and extraordinary meetings of a company.

Usually, however, it is not advisable to invest in the stock market through the shares. The best way to start investing in the stock market is to focus on derivative contracts that have underlying shares. In this way, you get the advantage of increasing earnings and, above all, earning both when stocks go down and when they go up, obviously making the right prediction.

How to Learn How to Play in the Stock Market

The best way to start is options. These derivative instruments are straightforward to use and understand. Binary trading is pretty easy: if we choose as a stock listed on a World Exchange (one of the main ones, of course), we only have to indicate whether the price of the asset will be increased or decreased at the end of a period. It does not count the level of variation, and only the sign counts: and this is perfect for learning because the aspiring trader can concentrate only on a few fundamental factors, leaving out all the details. It must be said that options trading can produce profits so high that many traders are choosing to trade options only, although they do not need a simplified approach.

Getting Started with Brokers

As a starting trader, your broker will be essential to you. Not just because you will want one with the lowest cost per trade, but also because you want the best research tools available to you. I highly recommend that you start with EOption Review – this brokerage house has the lowest transaction cost per option bought or sold and will be extremely useful when making the most profit off of trading a small number of options. Assuming that since you are at the beginner level and your entire investment fund is not all that large, the brokerage fees can add up quite quickly, and so this is an excellent firm for starting with small trades. For the best research tools available, you will want to go with Charles Schwab Review. This is a broker that you might never even want to trade through, but rather make an account, keep some money there, and use their tools for finding the most up to date prices/indexes for different options.

Their tools feature several neat applications, like predictions on what the cost of options will be a few months down the line based on assumptions that a trader input. This is not an account that you need to create right away but is one that will almost certainly be useful to you in the future as you continue to trade. Aside from these two brokerage houses, you will have lots of different choices for picking a broker. I recommend just dealing with these two to start, and even from these, you will probably want to avoid Charles Schwab as you find your way and make a few trades first.

These are indexes that list the most frequently purchased options, giving lots of information about the volume of options being sold, how they are being written, and when most of them are expected to expire. The essential piece of information will be the bid and ask price for options. The asking price is what option sellers are trying to get for selling one contract. The bid price is what buyers are willing to pay for an option. We refer to the split between them as the spread of the option. This concept may sound complicated, but the premise is quite easy when taken with an example. Suppose that you were interested in purchasing a call option from McDonald's. Don't worry about the strike price, expiration date, or exercise price. All you need to know is that you want to buy a call and that you know the underlying commodity is McDonald's stock. You would refer to an index on your broker's website, or refer to an index from one of the significant listing boards, such as the Chicago Board Options

Exchange, here you would find a listing of bid prices, asking prices, and the spread between them. These are typically listed in a per-share metric, such that if you wanted to buy one option contract, you would usually be multiplying the ask or bid price by one hundred to get the real cost of the option. This is because options are sold and bought measuring against 100 shares for each option contract. In this case, with the McDonald's stock, the bid price is $4.90, and the asking price is $5.12. The spread, in this case, is then $0.22. What this means is that a buyer is willing to buy an option on McDonald's stock for $4.90 per share, while a seller is willing to sell an option for $5.12 per share. You will also get a listing of the volume of the number of contracts traded in the last time interval (ranges depending on how you sort the options).

    The spread is useful because it tells you how much you would immediately lose per share if you bought an option on McDonald's and quickly turned around and sold it. In this case, you would be purchasing an option for $0.22 more than you would be selling the option, netting you the loss of that spread per share on buying the McDonald's option. There is a lot of useful information to be gleaned from the bid/ask price, as well as the spread for options contracts. First, it tells an options trader how the supply and demand of a particular option contract match each other, so that if the spread is quite large, there is either more need for an option or it is in limited supply. Two, it tells the options trader how much they could realistically write options for on a particular commodity. Three, and most important to both options traders and general investors, it shows the possible direction of a commodity in the near future.

    If the spread is quite large on McDonald's and the volume of calls is quite low, this means that investors believe the stock is due for a reversal shortly. The lack of options being sold signals that there is a discrepancy in the number of options being offered versus the number of opportunities that exist. In simplest terms, you can think of these three metrics, bid, ask, and spread, as a way of determining the supply and demand for options on a particular commodity. It will be one of the most useful indexes when learning what products to write or buy options for. How you use the information is highly variable on the volume of options sold, whether it is a call or put and other information about how a company is doing. It is not the end of all tools for determining the direction that a commodity will move, but it is instead just one tool among many.

In searching for options, you will find that indexes list a lot of additional information in addition to the end date, call or put, etc. The lists show metrics for the changes in the overall cost of the option. This is based on the spread of the option overall, with the essential parameters showing different ways in which the range has changed over time. This is highly variable based on where you are looking up an index, but most of the time they will have standard information like the percentage change in spread and volume of options for this date being sold.

It is essential that as you are searching for options, you are doing so knowing that there are thousands of options for each company listed every month. Listing an option to be sold is simple enough but buying one that will profit you takes some time getting used to. It is for this reason that I highly suggest doing plenty of searching on the brokerage firm of your choice before you start making any purchases. It can be a bit confusing to read listings at first, but a few searches and you'll get the hang of it.

As a final note, nearly all options are listed in the cost of the option per share. For example, a call for Starbucks may be recorded as $1.10. The exact price of this option is $110 because the choice must be purchased in increments of 100 shares. Also, since you may not be buying the option from the same trader, the call on the second hundred shares is likely to be a different price. It means that looking at the real value of price per share cannot just be extrapolated to 200 or 1000 shares. You have to figure that the prices are highly flexible and will not remain the same as you increase the number of calls or puts that you buy of any one company.

Size of Investment Fund & Amount to invest: The size of your investment fund is going to vary depending on how much you want to put at stake for your options trading future. I make the recommendation that you do not start with an amount of less than $2,000. Any amount more than this is excellent, but this is the absolute minimum that you will need to get started.

An ideal amount is closer to 4k or 5k. At these sums, your investment in each option can be quite sizeable, with good returns on trades that work well in your favor. It is critical that for each trade you make you risk no more than ten percent of your total investment fund. This is the upper limit of how much you will want to spend on a single option. You should never be paying more than this percentage on an only choice because if a trade goes poorly, it limits your ability to spread out risk in the future. Starting at $2,000, this means that each business you make should be limited to $200. You will find that there are not that many trades that you can conduct with that much money.

How Prices are Determined

Pricing is a complex subject when it comes to options trading. Not only is the price of an option based on the value of the asset, there are other external factors that have influence.

As an options trader, you want to make sure that you maximize your efforts to make a profit. Learning how to determine the prices you should pay for options is one of the basic ways that you can ensure that your yield is as high as it can be. You do not want to be stiffed by paying higher premiums than you should.

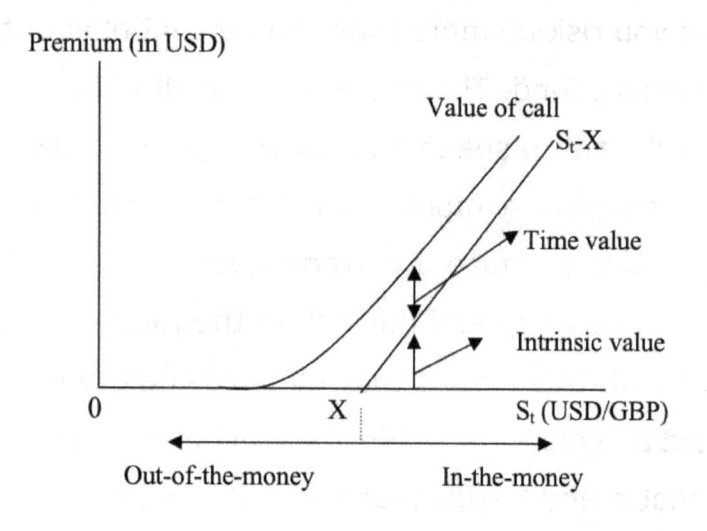

Pricing of options are determined by several factors.

The Value of the Asset

The effect this has on options prices is straightforward. If the value of this asset goes down, then exercising the option to sell becomes more valuable while the right to buy is become less valuable.

On the other hand, if the value increases, the right to sell it becomes less valuable while the right to buy it becomes more appealing due to this increase.

The Intrinsic Value

When an options trader pays a premium, this sum represents two values. The premium is made up of the intrinsic value, which is the current value of the option and the potential increase in value that this option can obtain over time. This potential increase over time is known as the time value.

The intrinsic value is how much money the option is currently worth. It represents what the buyer would receive if he or she decided to exercise the option at the current time.

Intrinsic value is calculated by determining the difference in the current price of an asset and a strike price of the option.

For an option to have an intrinsic value of zero, the option must be out of money. Therefore, the buyer would not exercise the option because this would result in a loss. The common strategy here is allowing the option to expire so that no pay off is made. As a result, the intrinsic value results in nothing to the buyer.

For a buyer to be in the money, the intrinsic value has to be greater than the premium to increase the value of the option. This place the buyer in a position to make a profit. The intrinsic value of for in the money for call options and put options are calculated slightly different. The formulas are as follows:

In the money call options

Price of Asset - Strike Price = Intrinsic Value

In the money put option

Strike Price - Price of Asset = Intrinsic Value

Intrinsic Value Formula

$$\text{Intrinsic Value of Business} = \frac{FCFE_1}{(1+r)^1} + \frac{FCFE_2}{(1+r)^2} + \cdots + \frac{FCFE_n}{(1+r)^n} + \frac{\text{Terminal Value}}{(1+r)^n}$$

$$\text{Intrinsic Value of Stock} = \frac{\text{Intrinsic Value Business}}{\text{No. of Outstanding Shares}}$$

The Time Value

This value is the additional amount an investor is willing to contribute to the premium of an option in addition to the intrinsic value. This willingness stems from the belief that an option will increase in value before the expiration date reaches. Typically, an investor is only willing to put forth this extra amount if the option expires months away. There would be little to no change in the value of an option in a few days.

The time value is calculated by finding the difference between the intrinsic value of an option and the premium. The formula looks like this:

Option Premium - Intrinsic Value = Time Value

Therefore, the total price of an option premium follows this formula:

Intrinsic Value + Time Value = Option Premium

Both time value and intrinsic value help traders understand the value of what they are paying for if they decide to purchase an option. While the intrinsic value represents the worth of the option if the buyer were to exercise it at the current time, the time value represents the possible future value before or on the expiration date. These two values are important because they help traders understand the risk versus the reward of considering an option.

Volatility

This describes how likely a price change will occur during a specified amount of time on the financial market. If a financial market is nonvolatile then the prices change very slowly or remain totally unaffected over a specific amount of time. Volatile markets, on the other hand, have fast-changing prices over short periods of time.

Fund Net Asset Value

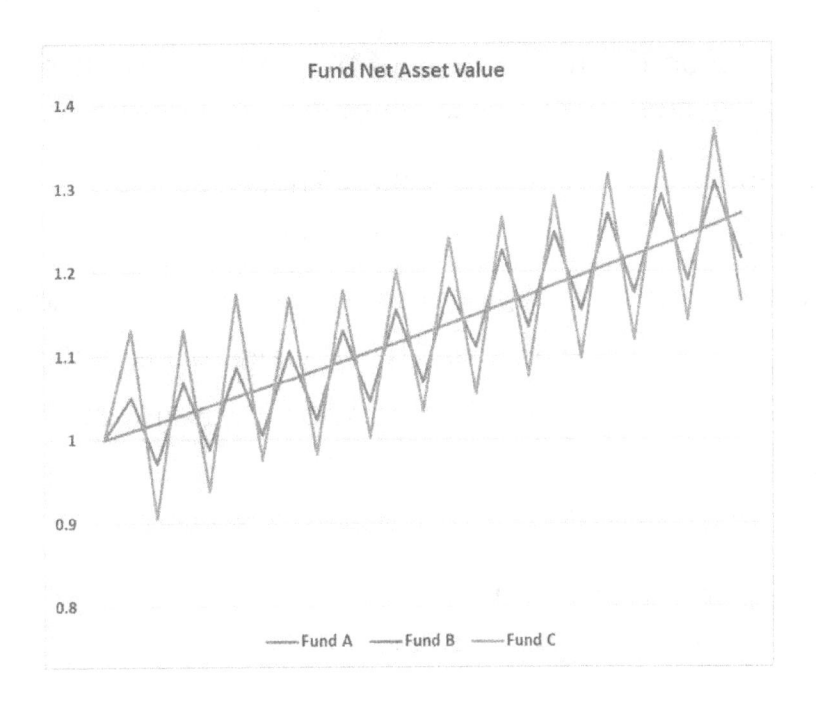

Option traders can make use of a financial market's volatility to get a higher yield for their investment in the future. Options traders normally avoid slow-changing financial markets because these non-volatile markets often mean that no potential profit is available to the trader. Therefore, option traders thrive on volatility even though volatility increases the risk of option trading. As a result, an options trader needs to know how to read the financial market correctly to know which options are likely to yield the highest returns. This ability comes with experience, continuous learning and keeping up to date on the happenings of the financial markets.

There are many factors that affect the volatility of a financial market. These factors include politics, national economics and news reports. Options traders typically use one of two options strategies to gain the best yield from volatile markets. They are called straddle strategy and the strangle strategy.

Interest Rates

Most people are familiar with the term interest rates. Interest rates apply to mortgages bank accounts and more. Interest rates as it applies to option trading is slightly different from the common variations.

The interest rate is defined as the percentage of a particular rate for the use of money lent over a period of time. This interest rate of an option has different effects on the call option and put option. The premiums for call options rise when interest rates rise and fall when interest rates fall. The effect is the opposite on puts options. The premiums for put options fall when interest rates rise and rise when interest rates fall.

Interest rates affect the time value of options no matter what category they fall in!

You will come across the term risk-free interest rate many times in your study of options trading. This is described as the return made on an investment with no loss of capital. This is a misleading term because all investments carry some level of risk, no matter how minute. This more serves as a parameter in options pricing models such as the Black-Scholes Model to determine the premium that should be paid.

Dividends

Dividends are distributions of portions of a company's profit at a specified period. This distribution must be decided and managed by the board of directors of a company. It is paid to a particular class of shareholders. Dividends can be distributed in the form of cash, shares of stock and other types of property. Exchange-traded funds and mutual funds also pay out dividends.

As it relates to options trading, options do not actually pay dividends. However, the associated assets attached to that option can have them and thus, options trader can receive those dividends if he or she exercises that option and takes ownership of those particular assets. While both call and put options can be affected by the presence of dividends of the associated asset, this effect on the types of options is widely varied. While the presence of dividends makes call options less expensive due to the anticipation of a drop-in price, it makes put options more expensive because the price will be decreased by the amount of the dividend.

Strategies for Beginners

There is a common misconception that trading options is inherently riskier than trading stocks. It's easy to see where this misconception comes from: many people do indeed trade options in a reckless manner. Options can be used to magnify returns on the upside, and the downside. In inexperienced or greedy hands, this can be a recipe for disaster.

Most of these reckless traders are buying options. The strategy that you are about to learn involves selling options.

Here's how it works:

You buy a stock, and then enter into a contract

("you sell some call options"). This contract says that you will get paid some cash today (the "premium"), in exchange for giving up the stock's potential upside past a certain point. Maybe you buy 100 shares of stock XYZ at 20.00 and agree to give up all potential upside past 21.00 ("the strike price"). In exchange, you get paid $1.00 per share (or $100, since you own 100 shares).

Let's go back to what just happened: you bought a stock at 20.00 and immediately got paid 1.00. In effect, you have only paid 19.00 for the stock.

If the stock goes to zero the next day, you lose 19.00 (or $1,900 since you own 100 shares). On the other hand, if you had bought the stock without entering into the contract, and the stock went to zero the next day, you would have lost 20.00 (or $2,000 since you own 100 shares).

Hopefully this shows how covered calls can actually decrease the risk of a long stock position.

So, what are the risks associated with covered calls?

Risk #1: Lost upside
Risk #2: See risk #1

The riskiest thing about covered calls is that you miss out on a stock's appreciation past a certain point.

If you sold covered calls on Apple (AAPL) back when it was $100 (pre-split) and then it ran up past $800, you left a pretty big chunk of change on the table.

But what if instead you held General Electric (GE) in your account over the past 2 years? (I'm writing this in May 2015.) You have watched the stock bounce between 23 and 28, pretty much going nowhere. You've been paid a small dividend while you waited but have otherwise been treading water. In this case, selling covered calls on the position would have generated significantly higher returns.

The moral?

Don't apply the covered calls strategy to stocks that you think will appreciate sharply in the near future.

Covered calls work best on stocks that are trading sideways, or slightly up.

If you own a stock in your long-term portfolio, and you don't think it is going anywhere over the short term, covered calls are an excellent strategy to generate some monthly income while you wait.

A Step-by-Step Guide to Selling Covered Calls

First, let's go over some basic terminology.

A "call option" (or just a "call") is a contract that gives you the right to buy a stock at a certain price, over a certain period of time, until the option expires. If you own a call option ("are long a call"), you have the right to buy the stock, but you don't have to buy the stock.

So, for example, let's look at a KO June 41.00 call.

"KO" is simply the ticker of the underlying stock, in this case, Coke ("The Coca-Cola Company").

"June" is what is called the option's "expiration date." This is the month when the options contract expires. Expiration usually occurs at the end of the day on the 3rd Friday of the month, or 19 June 2015 in this case.

"41.00" is the "strike price": this is the price at which the owner of the call option has the right to purchase the stock (or "call it away" from its owner, hence the name "call").

If you buy a call ("if you are long a call"), you are betting that the stock will move up in price.

If you sell a call ("if you are short a call"), you are betting that the stock will stay roughly where it is or move down in price.

If you sell a call, and the underlying stock moves up a lot in price, you can lose a lot of money, and end up having to buy back the call at a higher price. If you are just short a call, it is called a "naked call." It is a naked call because you are "exposed" to sharp up moves in the stock.

Covered calls are much safer.

When trading covered calls, we buy a stock and then sell an equivalent amount of call options at a strike price that is just above where we bought the stock. If the stock moves up sharply, you will lose money on the short call position, but you will make back an equal amount on the long stock position. In other words, you are "covered" and don't have the huge risk of loss that you do with naked calls.

For now, you should stick to covered calls.

Let's look at a real example to make this clear.

As I'm writing this, Coke (KO) is trading at

$40.94 per share.

I like Coke at this price, and so I decide to sell covered calls on it.

To make the numbers easy, let's assume that I have enough money to buy 1,000 shares of Coke.

If you are trading a small account ($5,000 or less), there is a special way of doing covered calls that you can learn about here:

So, if I have the capital, I buy 1,000 shares at 40.94. This costs me $40,940, plus a $4.95 commission (if you're using TradeKing), for a grand total of $40,944.95.

Now I immediately decide to sell calls against this stock position.

To get an options quote, I navigate to Yahoo Finance, enter the symbol KO, then click on "Options" in the left-hand menu.

Next, I go to the drop-down menu for the date, and select June 12, 2015, which is about 30 days from today.

I choose the strike price that is just above my purchase price: this strike price is 41.00.

I've already chosen an expiration date from the drop-down: June 12, 2015. This is the date that the contract ends ("expires").

Here's what it looks like on Yahoo Finance today. If you'd like to expand the image, just double-click on it:

[Yahoo Finance screenshot showing The Coca-Cola Company (KO) at 40.94 with call option chain for June 12, 2015. The strike price 41.00 and bid price 0.57 are circled.]

I've circled the strike price ("41") as well as the bid price ("0.57"). The bid is the price that the market is willing to pay for a call option. Since I am selling calls, I should set my limit order to the bid price, if I would like my order to be filled right away.

Each call option covers 100 shares of stock. So, if I now own 1,000 shares of Coke, I need to sell 10 (1,000 divided by 100) call options.

So, I sell 10 call options to the bid (use the order type "sell to open"), and my order is filled. If I used TradeKing, I was charged a commission of $4.95 base rate plus 10 contracts times $0.65 per contract, or $11.45. I sold 10 calls, and so my account was credited with 10 calls times 100 shares per call times 0.57 (the price at which I sold the calls), or $570.

My net credit after the commission is $570.00 minus $11.45, or $558.55.

I get to keep this $558.55 ("the premium") no matter what happens.

I am still long the 1,000 shares of Coke that I bought.

And I am "short" 10 call options in my account. I am "short" because I sold something that I didn't have. Don't worry about this for now.

As the price of the stock trades up, the shares of Coke will gain in value, while the short call position loses roughly an equal amount.

As the price of the stock trades down, the shares of Coke will lose value, while the short call position will make money.

As we mentioned before, covered calls work best in a flat to slightly up market.

Straddles and Strangles

Straddles and strangles are the most basic, intermediate trading strategies when it comes to options, and they are fascinating to execute. Almost every professional option trader loves them thanks to the high levels of neutrality and arbitrage they enable.

For those of you who are unfamiliar with the concept, arbitrage refers to taking advantage of price mismatches in the same product between two different markets. These days true arbitrage opportunities are rare but using options, you can implement this wonderful strategy to produce risk-free returns.

Let's look at a straddle first.

Long Straddles

The straddle is a true arbitrage strategy at heart. One of the key aspects of any arbitrage strategy is that the trader implementing it does not care which direction the price moves in. All they are concerned with is the degree of movement. The greater the degree of movement, the greater the profit.

This strategy is best used prior to times of high volatility. For example, if a company has a significant earnings announcement that is going to send its stock rocketing or cratering, but you don't know which way it is going to go, a straddle is the strategy for you.

Execution

The trade has two legs to it:

At the money long call

At the money long put

The idea is that prior to a volatility producing announcement, the stock price is going to move pretty violently in a given direction. The thing to note about a straddle is that it creates a range within which the trade will be unprofitable, so it isn't entirely risk-free. Let's see how this works.

AMZN is currently trading at $1833.51 and let's say there's some news due to come out in a week which is going to cause it to go either up or down massively. The closest at the money call and put are the ones at 1832.5 and 1835. The interesting thing, in this case, is that the 1835 put is in the money while the 1832.50 call is in the money. There isn't any at the money price for AMZN, so how do we work around this?

Well, you could choose 1835 as your price. The call is technically out of the money, but given the proximity to the market price, this isn't a huge risk. You could also choose 1832.50 as the strike price and buy an out of the money put instead of 1835. For this example, let's stick with 1835 as our preferred strike price. Given the timing of the announcement, purchasing front-month options is the best bet since near month and beyond options will likely have more volatility appended to them.

In AMZN's case, here's how the numbers look:

Cost of long call = $39.50

Cost of long put = $34.70

Total cost of trade entry = $74.20

The cost of the premiums is what creates a range around our strike price. In other words, the price needs to move beyond at least this hurdle to generate a profit. So, in this case, our range extends from $1800.30 to $1874.50. In other words, it needs to move by at least 2.1% to breakeven.

The key to getting a long straddle right is to get in on the action before the volatility is priced into the option. In AMZN's case, you can see that the number of points it needs to move is not that much. In real-life situations, as the event approaches, it is not uncommon to see points of at least 20%. Keeping an eye on this percentage before earnings yields is often a great indicator of volatility.

Ideally, you want to get in on the stock before the volatility is priced into it, but this is not always possible. There are two ways to screen for stocks that are good straddle candidates. Both the approaches are realistic and don't involve you trying to dig for insider information to get in before the volatility gets priced in.

First, pay attention to those stocks which have high volatility priced into their options. If there's an upcoming event, you can bet there's a good chance that the stock is going to do something. A basket of these stocks will produce a decent amount of returns on a yearly basis. I say decent because you cannot expect to hit home runs with this method. There will be some that won't break the range and some that will. Over the long run, the odds are good that you will make good money on this.

The next method requires more research and will result in a lesser number of candidates, but those that do make themselves available will be home runs for sure. The idea is to find stocks that have mispriced options. Often, the Black Scholes model underestimates the volatility that will be produced in events which are far beyond the standard deviation norms for volatility.

For example, a reliable company in a tough sector failing to meet earnings expectations can be classified as a two-sigma event, meaning it is two standard deviations away from the norm. Black Scholes has problems with estimating volatility for events that are 5-6 sigma away. Such events have never occurred in financial models but happen all the time in real life. Hence, the model dependent formula has no way to account for them.

In bigger stocks, this weakness is well known, and you will find traders jumping in and the premium adjusting itself well. However, in smaller stocks, this does not happen because institutional traders do not trade them too much, thanks to the negligible impact they'll have on their overall profit numbers.

A good example of such an event might be a lawsuit that threatens the company's entire existence. If the lawsuit goes against it, the stock will go plausibly to zero. If not, it should go back to the levels it was at before the event began, which will be many magnitudes higher. You will always find that the options in such situations will be mispriced and that a straddle will generate huge profits because the degree to which the market will move will far outstrip the straddle range.

Short Straddles

While long straddles help you take advantage of huge price movements, short straddles let you take advantage of close to no movement. In other words, the exact opposite environment is taken advantage of. I'm mentioning this here only for information purposes because traders will often run into this term when reading more about the topic.

Generally, you should stay away from short straddles until you've made some money and built your skill levels up first. They are a more advanced trading tactic, and it is unlikely your broker will let you execute them unless you have some credibility.

Long Strangles

Much like a long straddle aims to take advantage of a burst of volatility in a stock, the long strangle has the same goal but aims to do it at a much lower cost. While the straddle requires you to buy options with the same strike price, the strangle spreads it out a bit and creates a band between the strike prices of both legs.

Let's look at this in more detail.

Execution

The trade has two legs to it:

A long out of the money call

A long out of the money put

Given that you will be buying out of the money options, your cost of entry is going to be lesser than that of a straddle. However, the degree to which price needs to jump is going to be greater. In some cases, it is possible to end up with the same range as a straddle with a strangle, but this is a time-consuming exercise and beginners are better off focusing on execution.

The range size is just the distance to the strike price in either direction added to the premium paid for each option leg.

Also, just like there exists a short straddle, a short strangle exists as well. Beginners are better off building their skills before dabbling in this strategy.

This brings to a close our look at combination strategies. Given that they fall into the realm of more advanced strategies, I'm not keen on spending time on them since it might detract from the strategy that we've already talked about. As you can see, there is a range of strategies for you to use and employ in the markets. Take the time to get to know them.

However, before you get to know them well, you need to understand the basics of the market environment.

Beginners' Common Mistakes

Trading options are more involved than trading stocks, so there are ample opportunities to make mistakes. It's important to take the approach of going small and slow at first so that you don't lose the shirt off your back. That said, if you run into mistakes don't get too down about it. Dust yourself off and get up to fight another day. With that said, let's have a look at some common mistakes and how to avoid them.

Putting All Your Eggs In One Basket

While there is a difference between investing and trading, as traders can learn a few things from our investor brothers (and most people are a little of both anyway). Don't let everything ride on one trade. If you take all the money, you have and invest it in buying options for one stock, you're making a big mistake. Doing that is very risky, and as a beginning trader, you're going to want to mitigate your risk as much as possible. Betting on one stock may pay off sometimes, but more times than not it's going to lead you into bankruptcy territory.

Investing More Than You Can

It's easy to get excited about options trading. The chances to make fast money and the requirements that you analyze the markets can be very enticing. Oftentimes that leads people into getting more excited than they should. A good rule to follow with investing is to make sure that you're setting aside enough money to cover living expenses every month, with a security fund for emergencies. Don't bet the farm on some sure thing by convincing yourself that you'll be able to make back twice as much money and so cover your expenses. Things don't always work out.

Going All in Before You're Ready

Another mistake is failing to take the time to learn options trading in real time. Just like getting overly excited can cause people to bet too much money or put all their money on one stock, some people are impatient and don't want to take the time to learn the options markets by selling covered calls. It's best to start with covered calls and then move slowly to small deals buying call options. Leave put options until you've gained some experience.

Failure to Study the Markets

Remember, you need to be truly educated to make good options trades. That means you'll need to know a lot about the companies that you're either trying to profit from or that you're shorting. Options trading isn't possible without some level of guesswork, but make your guesses educated guesses, and don't rely too much on hunches.

Not Getting Enough Time Value

Oftentimes, whether you're trading puts or calls, the time value is important. A stock may need an adequate window of time in order to beat the stock price whether it's going above it or plunging below it. When you're starting out and don't know the markets as well as a seasoned trader, you should stick to options you can buy that have a longer time period before expiring.

Not Having Adequate Liquidity

Sometimes beginning investors overestimate their ability to play the options markets. Remember that if you buy an option, to make it work for you- you're going to need money on hand to buy stocks when the iron is hot. And you're going to need to buy 100 shares for every option contract. Before entering into the contract, make sure that you're going to be able to exercise your option.

Not Having a Grip on Volatility

If you don't understand volatility and its relation to premium pricing, you may end up making bad trades.

Failing to Have a Plan

Trading seems exciting, and when you're trading, you may lose the investors mentality. However, traders need to have a strategic plan as much as investors do. Before trading, make sure that you have everything in place, including knowing what your goals are for the trades, having pre-planned exit strategies, developing criteria for getting into a trade so that you're not doing on a whim or based on emotion.

Ignoring Expiration Dates

It sounds crazy, but many beginners don't keep track of the expiration date. Would you hate to see a stock go up in price, and then hope it keeps going up, and it does, only to find out that your expiration date passed before you exercised your option?

Overleveraging

It's easy to spend huge amounts of money in small increments. This is true when it comes to trading options. Since stocks are more expensive, it's possible to get seduced by purchasing low priced options. After all, options are available at a fraction of the cost that is required to buy stocks. And you might keep on purchasing them until you're overleveraged.

Buying Cheap Options

In many cases, buying cheap things isn't a good strategy. If you're buying a used car, while you might occasionally find a great car that is a good buy, in most cases a car is cheap for a reason. The same applies to options trading. When it comes to options, a cheap premium probably denotes the option is out of the money. Sure, you save some money on a cheap premium, but when the expiration date comes, you might see the real reason the option contract was a cheap buy. Of course, as we described earlier, there may be cases where cheap options have the capacity to rebound and become profitable by the time the expiry date arrives. But taking chances like that is best left to experienced traders.

Giving in to Panic

Remember that you have the right to buy or sell a stock if you've purchased an option. Some beginners panic and exercise their right far too early. This can happen because of fears that they'll be missing out an opportunity with a call option, or because of fears that a stock won't keep going down on a put.

Not Knowing How Much Cash You Can Afford to Lose

Going into options trading blindly is not a smart move. With each option trade you make, you need to have a clear idea of how much cash you have on hand to cover losses and exercising your options. You'll also want to know how much cash you can afford to lose if things go south.

Jumping into Puts Without Enough Experience and Cash to Cover Losses

Remember if you're selling puts, you will have to buy the stock at the strike price if the buyer exercises their option. This is a huge risk. The stock could have plunged in value, and you're going to have to buy the stock at the strike price, possibly leaving you with huge losses. Don't go into selling puts with your eyes closed, in fact, beginners are better off avoiding selling puts. But if you must do it, make sure you can absorb the losses when you bet wrong.

Piling it On

Most beginner mistakes are related to panic. If you're looking at losses on options, some beginners double and triple up hoping to make it up when things turn better. Instead, they end up losing more money. Instead of giving in to panic, learn when to cut your losses and re-evaluate your trading strategy.

Staying in a Written Contract When You Should Get Out

If you've sold an option and it's looking like you might face a loss, you can always get out of it by selling.

Chapter 4. Rules for Successful Trading of Options

In order to succeed in the world of options trading, you are required to trade by following certain rules and tips. All the tips that you will be finding here can help you to achieve all that you wish to have in trading. Mistakes are meant to be made when you first start with trading. So, let's have a look at some of the basic rules of options trading and try your best to avoid mistakes.

Having Knowledge About the Time for Improvising the Plan

One of the most important aspects that are needed for successful trading is having a proper plan. But, besides that, you are also needed to take care of one more thing, and that is the perfect time for improvising your plans. There will be several instances when you will have to shift away from the plan. Your emotional aspects might also not work in such instances. To be successful in the world of options trading, you need to have proper knowledge regarding the time of the plan when it will be losing its validity. As you create a proper plan for trading, it can help you to set up a valid path for you. But, as you set up the path for yourself, that does not indicate you will be moving by the same path blindly right to the end of the world. Every trader needs to pass through a point of time in their trading career when everything seems to go out of hand. This will ultimately be making the proper plan to turn into something completely useless for that specific situation.

    That is why, when you are having the thoughts of designing a new plan, you need to identify all its weak points. As you are the one who is creating all trading plans, you will have proper knowledge when it can actually fail. The conditions of the trading market will keep on changing. So, what you have planned might work today but will not be the same the other day. If you are trying to keep on following your plan of action that has been predetermined even if the market condition gets turned 360-degree, you will be making a big mistake. When you keep on following a fixed plan of action, you are most likely to fail. You will surely need a lot of practice to understand the market scenario. The conditions will keep on changing. But, as you take a small step in the right direction, you can call it progress. This also consists of being aware of the major differences that come between the present situation and the situation tomorrow.

Avoiding Trades That Are Out-of-the-Money

With the help of certain strategies, you can surely generate some amount of profit by purchasing out-of-the-money call options. But, such trades are only a few in numbers and can be treated as exceptions. As you enter the options trading world, you are most likely to get attracted like a magnet to the call options of out-of-the-money. In fact, it is very natural. The main reason behind this is that such options are affordable and cheap than the others.

But, you are also required to keep one thing in mind: the stock market and options market are different from one another. Even when you dedicate all your attention to the underlying security while buying options, that cannot be taken as a good strategy. It won't be a great idea if you are willing to purchase low and then sell them out as high. As a call option tends to be out-of-the-money, the chances of the same rising up again to the required levels before the expiry date are very low. So, if you are willing to purchase options of this nature, you will be doing nothing but gamble with all that you have.

Preparing the Entry and Exit Plan Before Starting

Trading of options is all about finding out the perfect positions of entry and exit. You are required to learn this thing first in the proper way before you start trading. No matter what kind of techniques you will be using for the adjustment, nothing can actually rectify a bad entry point. This might even result in you incurring a huge loss. But, there is something more important in options trading than fixing the proper entry and exit points. Do you have any idea what exactly it is? It is the knowledge of the fact that you need to exercise the entry and exit points much before you have given in all your capital.

Most of the beginner options traders have the notion that every trade they are going to make will bring them huge amounts of profits. They give in their all for making the best out of the last cent spent by them. But, if you really want to succeed as a trader in the world of options, you cannot start following this idea. When you just aim to bring in huge amounts of profits, it can bring in new obstacles to your path. Until and unless you have a proper plan related to trading that can bring in profits as well, you will be performing a number of trades that can develop small profits. So, when you fix up your mind to stick to only one specific trade as if it is the only one left, you will actually be doing wrong. It will be resulting in huge losses for you.

So, once you have gained a potential amount of small profits from various trades, there is no need to think about the same again. You are only required to protect all that you have made. Of course, you can ignore this suggestion and keep on trading with your own trading plans. It can bring you more potential profits as well. But, the fact is that the loss you will be incurring will be much more than the actual profit. You might lose all your profit without even getting the chance to use it properly.

Not Trading for Wealth

If you think of options trading in a way that the returns you will be getting will be more than 150% or so, it will be better for you if you just step back and try to reconsider your position. It is true that there are certain investments that can bring in huge amounts of profits. But, all the trades that you are going to make will not be the same. Various options traders think that options trading will be making them rich in one night. But, in reality, nothing actually happens like that.

In case you have opted for options trading to generate wealth, you have made up a wrong notion about the trading of options. Options trading is all about working with the perfect strategy to make sure of daily income flow. As you try to be hungry for grabbing huge profits, there are chances that you will be overseeing the risky aspects. Never forget that options trading is very risky in nature. If you take one wrong step, all that you have can vanish in a second.

Risk in Options Trading

Risk is at the heart of all types of investment as without it there would be need for reward. As such, options trading is risky at the best of times, even for those who might be considered experts and certainly for those who are still new to the field. Luckily, there are certainly ways to mitigate that risk as many of the major pitfalls of options trading have been well documented by those who have come before. What's more, they have also been distilled down and classified so that all you need to do is memorize the following and ensure that you do your best not to let it intrude on your trading success.

It doesn't matter what type of trade you are working with, the first thing you are going to want to do is to take three main things into consideration. First, you will want to be aware of how much a specific price is likely going to change prior to the expiration of the option in question. From there, you will want to determine how volatile the underlying asset is as well as how much time the option has to turn you a profit prior to its expiration. When you are purchasing options, it is important also to identify the direction you expect the underlying stock to move in as well as how long you expect it to continue to move in the specified direction. In these instances, the amount of time that is still available won't be as important when it comes to ensuring the overall maximum value.

To ensure that you minimize risk, it is important to keep in mind that the best strategies are those that focus on either high positive risk value or high negative risk value, there is little value in betting on the middle ground. Remember, some option types are always going to end up being more profitable than others in specific scenarios, you just need to have the patience and the foresight to know what's coming before it gets here. With that being said, however, it is important to always keep in mind that statistical projections cannot actually tell the future which means that any analysis that is done is strictly hypothetical. Never invest more money into a particular trade, no matter how reliable it seems, than you can ultimately afford to lose.

When it comes to making trades in groups, or combining them in other ways, it is important to consider the net risk of the entire trade instead of focusing on the specific risk likelihoods of parts of the whole. This will make it easier for you to determine the most profitable way to move forward at any juncture because it makes the risk/reward split much easier to analyze. Remember, there are multiple different types of risk which means that understanding what each means for your specific trade is crucial to covering all your bases and making success options trades on a reliable basis.

Delta:

Delta can be thought of as the amount of overall risk that you take on depending on how likely the underlying asset in question is going to move prior to the point where the option expires. If the asset is at the money at the moment, then the delta is going to be .5. What you can take from this is the fact that when the underlying asset moves a single point in either direction then the option will move .5 points. Puts are always going to have a delta of somewhere between -1 and 0 and calls will always have a delta that is somewhere between 1 and 0.

Delta should always be the first type of risk

that you consider as it will do the most to help you immediately determine if a specific trade is going to be in your best interest or not. You will find that it is the most helpful when it can be used to make decisions related to puts you are interested in making as it will help make it clear the direction the underlying asset is going to be likely to move in. To determine the delta, you are going to want to start by considering historical data related to the underlying assets by looking at previous strike prices in comparison to their comparable puts. When it comes to measuring delta, it is important to keep in mind that cheaper options are naturally going to have a lower delta. This occurs naturally as delta measures the chance an option will be profitable at expiration. This is why you are going always to want to avoid options with a delta that is either .4 or -.4 because it is rather unlikely that they are going to end up being favorable trades by the time everything is said and done.

Rho:

Rho is the name given to the quantity of risk that surrounds the interest rates relating to an underlying asset and the probable that changes in this area will result in changes to the underlying asset price and thus negatively affect the price of the option as well. As a general rule, you can expect interest rates to increase along with call prices, causing a decrease in put values. The reverse of this statement will also be true, causing an increase in put prices and a decrease in interest rates. Rho is going to be the most influential when the price of the underlying asset is greater than or equal to the option price. Calls will always have a positive Rho and puts will always have a negative rho. Rho is going to be relevant primarily those who are interested in options trading as a form of long-term investment.

Gamma:

If delta measures the amount of change that occurs between the underlying asset and the option in question, then gamma measures the likelihood that the delta is going to remain the same as long as the option remains active. The larger the gamma grows, the closer the underlying asset and the related option are likely to be to one another and a smaller gamma means that the variation between them is quite large because the stock has fallen beneath the strike point. Big gammas mean big profits but also larger degrees of risk. Additionally, you will want to keep in mind that the gamma will increase naturally as it gets closer to the point at which the option is going to expire. If you need to know just how much the gamma is likely to increase during this period you can certainly find out, all you need to do is consider the gamma of the gamma.

Theta:

Theta is a representation of the rate at which the time the option has left is currently expiring in comparted to how much time it has as a whole. Theta starts as a positive amount that starts to tick down the instant that an option comes into existence. Theta decreases at a steady rate compared to the price of the related option as it is guaranteed to lose value each second it ticks closer to expiration. A trade will remain profitable for the holder as long as delta remains greater than theta and will make money for the writer once this balance reverses itself.

As an options trader, it is important always to be aware of the fact that theta will constantly be changing, and that this change will increase in frequency the closer the option it is measuring gets to its expiration point. Theta is going to be the most important variable to consider if you are planning to make a trade based around the assumption that the market is not going to change prior to the options expiration. If this is not the case, then theta will be the least relevant element of risk to your trades as long as you work around it as needed.

Vega:

Vega is the type of risk that measure how volatile the underlying asset is compared to the market as a whole. Vega can be difficult to accurately determine at points, simply because it is possible to change despite the fact that the price of the asset it points to remained neutral during the same period. As such, making a successful options trade doesn't mean being able to avoid Vega completely, it means understanding how to take advantage of it regardless of the level of volatility that is in play.

Different options are going to respond in different ways to increasing Vega; those that respond positively are known as long volatility options and those that respond negatively are called short volatility options. Options that have a long volatility will have a positive amount of Vega and short volatility options are going to have a nega Vega. If you find an option with a neutral Vega then it will have a neutral level of volatility to go along with it.

Chapter 5. Risk Management

Quantitative and Qualitative

Risk management is both qualitative and quantitative. The quantitative bit is far easier to understand since it is just a matter of crunching numbers and monitoring a bunch of statistics with regards to your account. Now, if you were trading directionally, the number of metrics you need to monitor is enormous.

Thankfully, when it comes to options, you only need to track a few. Let's take a look at these.

Risk per Trade

More than anything else, it is your risk per trade that determines your success. Common wisdom is not to risk more than two percent of your capital per trade and in the case of options trading, this is correct. Directional trading requires you to risk far less than this in order to be successful.

The true measure of a good trader is how consistent they are in risking the same percentage of their account on each and every trade. A lot of beginners get on a winning streak at times and then start playing loose with this, only to be hit by a big loss that wipes out all their prior gains.

There is a school of thought that proposes that risking a fixed amount per trade, as opposed to a fixed percentage, is a better model. Suffice to say that, risking the same amount will bring you greater gains per trade and exaggerate your winning streaks but will do the same to your losses.

What's more, thanks to your losses being exaggerated, you'll have to keep making more and more gains to simply breakeven constantly and this will wipe out your account pretty soon since the basic math of all this is against you. Remember, you can't precisely predict the outcome of most trades in advance. Thus, it's best to risk the same percentage of your account every trade.

Win Percent

The win percentage of your strategy, that is the number of times you make money, is one half of an important measure that determines whether you'll make money or not. Usually, thanks to the way we've been brought up and have had UR performances measured in school, we chase the highest win percentages, thinking ninety percent is better than forty.

Well, in academia, this is true. However, in the chaotic world of the markets, this is far from the case. Making money on a trade is not about being right. You can be right about the markets and still lose money in the long run. This is best explained after we look at the second half of the equation.

Average Win Percent

Your average win percent is the amount of

money you win on average, when you do make money, expressed as a percentage of your account or as a multiple of the amount you risk per trade on average. So, if you risk R per trade, which might be 2% of your account, and if you make 4% on a win on average, you will make 2R per win.

The average win percent and the win percent together determine whether you'll make money or not. So out of ten trades, if you win two, a win rate of twenty percent, and your average win is 2R, you will not make money. This is because your eight losses will cost you 8R and your wins will only amount to 4R. This is a net loss of 4R.

However, if you make 5R on average per win, you will make money with a twenty percent win rate. In this case, your losses will add up to 8R as previously, but your wins will add up to 10R, giving you an overall profit of 2R. If you risk two percent of your account, this is a profit of 4% over ten trades.

Now if you manage to take two hundred trades over the course of a year, you'll be making 80% in a year. This is precisely what professional traders do make and it takes an extraordinarily high level of skill to hit such numbers. My point is that your profitability is determined by both numbers, not just a single one.

As you can see, it is perfectly possible to make money by being 'right' just twenty percent of the time. In a regular academic examination, this will guarantee your failure, but in the markets, it's just one half of an equation.

Strategy Evaluation

This gives us an excellent method of figuring out the profitability of strategies. If a strategy has a low win percent but high average win percent, it is perfectly valid to implement it, instead of trying to chase strategies that have high win percentages simply. For example, if you have the previously described strategy and another one with a 90%-win rate but only a 0.5R average win percent.

Over two hundred trades, the previous strategy makes 80% but this strategy, which is correct 90% of the time, will make you 35% over the same number of trades. So, which is the better strategy? The one where you have more losses or the one where you have more wins? Clearly, asking which one has more wins or loses is missing the point.

So, don't blindly chase high win rates or strategies that claim you won't lose even a single trade. For the rest of us, evaluating both the win percentage and the average win size as a function of the percent risk per trade is what determines whether or not a strategy is good.

Qualitative Risk

Let's say you settle down in front of your television on the weekend and switch on the TV to catch your favorite game. You're fully prepped and have your TV and assorted accessories set just so. Your friends have come over as well and all in all, it's a great atmosphere. There's just one problem: your team's star athlete, the one on whom the result of the game hinges, has turned up to the game hungover.

Now, it isn't unheard of such things to happen in pro sports, but when it does happen, you can imagine the reaction that follows. The athlete is roundly criticized as a buffoon, rightly so, and the sports media have a field day debating where he's about to be traded to next. We instinctively understand that preparation is the key to success and turning up hungover is hardly good preparation.

Yet, how many of us sit down to trade after having just walked in from work? We're tired and frustrated from whatever is going on in that world and think we can simply waltz in and make money in the markets. The very same markets that are full of professionals who make a living from it and are responsible for the management of many millions and billions.

Do you seriously think anyone can be successful trading this way? Do you think trading is simply a matter of learning the right strategies and then implementing it with the snap of a finger? If so, this is an indicator that your mindset is incorrect and that you don't understand what trading risk management involves.

Make no mistake; you will need to prepare and have your wits fully about you as you sit down to trade. You cannot afford any distractions like checking your smartphone or trying to wing something at the last minute. You need good sleep and need to exercise and eat well.

This is why I called the adrenaline-filled, coked-out atmosphere of trading floors in movies unrealistic because it is impossible to trade this way. A lot of beginners get seduced by this 'devil may care' type of depiction and try to do the same when it comes to their own hard-earned money. Needless to say, this results in a quick wipeout and the ones who will take their money are the traders who have prepared themselves.

You need to follow a specific mental and physical routine prior to operating in the markets. Meditation and other mental calming techniques are a great idea and will enable you to see things clearly, as they are. Also, avoid trading when things are not going well for you with your regular life.

There's no rule that says you have to trade each and every day of the year. Take adequate time to reflect on your skills and practice them well. Practice them so well that you know them by heart. The live market is not a place for you to be questioning whether the signal is valid or not. You simply need to pull the trigger and execute.

Sometimes, despite our best intentions, we fail to follow our plans. This is an indication that the problem is not so much with our technical strategy or risk but with our mindset.

Option Trader's Mindset

Options trading is most suitable for a certain personality type and mindset. But if you are intrigued by the concept of options, but you simply have not had a chance to develop the correct mindset before, there are a few tips that we can rely on to get in the right frame of mind.

You Can Weather the Storm

Options prices can move a lot throughout short periods. So, someone who likes to see their money protected and not losing any is not going to be suitable for options trading. Now, we all want to come out ahead, so I am not saying that you have to be happy about losing money to be an options trader. What you have to be willing to do is calmly observe your options losing money, and then be ready to stick it out to see gains return in the future. This is akin to riding a real roller coaster, but it is a financial roller coaster. Options do not slowly appreciate the way a Warren Buffett investor would hope to see. Options move big on a percentage basis, and they move fast. If you are trading multiple contracts at once, you might see yourself losing $500 and then earning

$500 over a matter of a few hours. In this sense, although most options traders are not "day traders" technically speaking, you will be better off if you have a little bit of a day trading mindset.

You Don't Make Emotional Decisions

Since options are, by their nature, volatile, and very volatile for many stocks, coming to options trading and being emotional about it is not a good way to approach your trading. If you are emotional, you are going to exit your trades at the wrong time in 75% of cases. You don't want to make any sudden moves when it comes to trading options. As we have said, you should have a trading plan with rules on exiting your positions, stick to those rules and you should be fine.

Be a Little Bit Math-oriented

To understand options trading and be successful, you cannot be shy about numbers. Options trading is a numbers game. That doesn't mean you have to drive over to the nearest university and get a statistics degree. But if you do understand probability and statistics, you are going to be a better options trader. Frankly, it's hard to see how you can be a good options trader without having a mind for numbers. Some math is at the core of options trading and you cannot get around it.

You are Market-focused

You don't have to set up a day trading office with ten computer screens so you can be tracking everything by the moment, but if you are hoping to set up a trade and lazily come back to check it three days earlier, that isn't going to work with options trading. You do need to be checking your trades a few times a day. You also need to be keeping up with the latest financial and economic news, and you need to keep up with any news directly related to the companies you invest in or any news that could impact those companies. If the news does come out, you are going to need to make decisions if it's news that isn't going to be favorable to your positions. Also, you need to be checking the charts periodically, so you have an idea of where things are heading for now.

Focus on a Trading Style

As you can see, there are many different ways that you can trade options. In my opinion, sticking to one or two strategies is the best way to approach options trading. I started off buying call options, but now, I focus on selling put credit spreads and iron condors. You should pick what you like best and also something that aligns with your goals. I moved into selling put credit spreads and iron condors because I became interested in the idea of making a living from options trading with regular income payments, rather than continuing to buy calls and hope that the share price would go up. There is no right or wrong answer, pick the trading style that is best suited to your style and needs.

Keep Detailed Trading Journals

It's easy to fool yourself when trading options, especially if you are a beginner. I hate to make the analogy, but this is kind of like going to the casino. If you have friends that gamble at casinos, then you are going to notice that they tend to remember the wins, and they will forget all the times that they gambled and lost. I had a cousin that won a boat, and she was always bragging about how she won a boat at the casino. I remember telling her that yes, she won a boat, but she paid $65,000 more than the boat was worth to the casino over the years. You don't want to get in the same situation with your options trading. It can be an emotional experience because trading options are active and fast-paced. When you have a profitable trade, it will be exciting. But you need to keep a journal to record all of your trades, to know exactly what the real situation is. That doesn't mean you quit if you look at your journal and find out you have a losing record, what you do is figure out why your trades aren't profitable and then make adjustments.

Options Traders are Flexible

I have said this before, but one thing you need to remember about options trading is you can make money no matter what happens to the stock. So, you need to avoid falling into the trap of only trading options to make money one way. Most frequently, people do what they have been brainwashed to do and they will trade call options hoping to profit from rising share prices. If you are in that mindset now, you need to challenge yourself and begin trading in different ways so that you can experience making money from declining stock prices, or in the case of iron condors, stock prices that don't even change at all. You need to be able to adapt to changing market conditions to profit as an options trader. So, don't entrap yourself by only using one method. Earlier, I said to use one or two styles, but you should be ready to branch out when market conditions change. Remember this – market conditions always change eventually. As I am writing, we are in the midst of a long-term bull market, but it won't last forever.

Take a Disciplined Approach

Don't just buy options for a certain stock because it feels good. You need to research your stocks. That will include doing fundamental analysis. This is going to mean paying attention to the history of a stock, knowing what the typical ranges are for, stock in recent history is, and also reading through the company's financial statements and prospectus. Remember, I suggest picking three companies to trade options on for a year and also two index funds.

The index funds require less research, but for the three companies that you pick, you should get to know those companies inside and out. Stick with them for a year, at the end of each year, evaluate each company. Then decide if you want to keep them and bring them forward into the following year's trades. If one company is not working out for you, then move on and try a different company.

Trading with LEAPS

Leaps are interesting options. They expire a year or more into the future. This is different than the short-term options that most people are trading. LEAPS are more expensive, but they can also represent money-making opportunities. LEAPS also give you an indirect way to control stock.

Profiting from LEAPS

LEAPS have high prices because they have a lot of extrinsic value. Looking at June 18, 2021, Facebook call options, the $195 call is priced at $42.13 a share. So that represents a $4,213 options contract. According to the chart, it made 3.4% today, which isn't a huge amount, but I challenge you to find a bank or mutual fund that has a return of 3.4% per day. The open interest is 133. This meets our minimum criteria for getting involved in a trade. It's quite small compared to Facebook options that expire in the following month, but it's enough open interest that it's going to be possible to get in and out of a trade in a reasonable amount of time. The implied volatility is a solid 33%. For comparison, the $195 call that expires in three weeks is priced at $12.48.

Although LEAPS are expensive, they have a lot of potential for profits. You can get into a LEAP and if the stock makes a solid move, you can close your position and make large amounts of money. For that $195 call that expires in June 2021, the delta is 0.64. That means that even though the option has a lot of extrinsic value since it expires a long way into the future, it's pretty sensitive to price changes in the stock that is with the option. If the share price goes up to $1, the option price will go up by $64. LEAPS don't suffer much from time decay. Theta for this option is only 0.03. If the share price goes up to $20 after an earnings call, the option is going to go up by $1,280. So, you can make pretty good profits. The barrier to entry is the high price to buy one.

Poor Mans Covered Call

One of the interesting things that you can do with a LEAP is you can use it to sell covered calls. That sounds crazy, but it works. You can use the LEAP to cover call options that you sell to open. So, you can invest in LEAPS at a fraction of what it costs to invest in the stock, and then start selling calls against the options to generate income. Although it might cost $4,600 to buy a Facebook LEAP, it would cost nearly $20,000 to buy 100 shares of stock. Buying a LEAP gives you de facto control over a hundred shares of stock at a much smaller price than the investment cost.

For the price of 100 shares of Facebook, you could invest in 4-5 LEAPS, and have a lot more room to work with as far as selling call options. So, you could end up having a higher income.

Chapter 6. Designing a Trading Plan Flexibility: Adapting Your Strategy to Market Conditions

The trader must never be obstinate, he must agree to adopt. This situation is obviously delicate. A good trader must rigorously apply his trading plan, while not considering the rules of the plan as immutable. Traders often apply the same strategy regardless of market configuration. The good trader considers the different market conditions and develops the most effective strategies for each situation. Thus, some day-traders have a strategy for opening, another for mid-day and finally one for closing. Others have adopted specific strategies for bull markets, bear markets and for trend-free markets. A good trader is able to adapt to changing markets and new conditions.

In addition, market conditions change over time (the market of the 2000s is different from that of the 1990s). Some effective strategies have not been effective today.

Nevertheless, the adaptation of the strategy must be based on in-depth research work and a critique of the methods used. The trader should never question his system when operating in real-time because it can be harmful. This phase of reflection should always be conducted calmly: the trader must prioritize strategic thinking before the fight and apply his strategy calmly in the heat of the moment.

Finally, for the great trader Mark Weinstein, "no approach in technical analysis works all the time. You have to know when to use each method. I do not believe in mathematical systems that approach markets in the same way. I use my person as the system and I constantly change the input to achieve the same output: profit."

The professional trader is constantly adapting its strategies to market conditions. He questions his system and tries to improve it with the aim of performance. Some principles are immutable, but it is still possible to improve certain rules or techniques of opening and closing positions, and this is what the big trader should be trying to do by being flexible and adapting himself to the evolution of the market.

Look For the Line of Least Resistance

The strategy must always stick to market circumstances. The trader must know the direction of the flows because it is by marrying that he dominates them. In trading, you should never oppose the course of things and respect the famous saying "trout is your ally". We must leave the market to dictate the procedure to follow and not pretend to want to impose our certainty.

Thus, when a market is without trend, it is dangerous to apply a trend tracking strategy. In this case, the trader will only have to buy support and sell resistance. The trader must pierce the intentions of his opponents, the object of the analysis. He must decipher the intentions of professional traders, including detecting the right signals and eliminating false signals.

Lessons Learned

A successful trader lets his profits run and quickly cuts his losses. As a result, it maximizes profits and minimizes losses and achieves gains on average greater than losses.

In low-performing traders, the average loss is usually greater than the average gain: they quickly exit their winning positions and return to hope mode when the market invalidates their point of view instead of facing reality. Everything seems linked: the successful trader has a high payoff ratio and an honorable probability of success, which allows him to take more risks and thus to record a superior performance.

Example of a Trading System

Suppose that the trader relies on the following criteria to open a position:

- To position himself only in the presence of a double-bottomed graphic figure;

- Bullish divergence on the validated RSI, - MACD higher than its signal line.

The trader has tested his system over quite a long history, and he finds that it has a probability of success of 60% and a payoff ratio of 2. It is a profitable system that can be used in the markets. Nevertheless, the probability of success, as well as the payoff ratio, is based on past data, which the trader will never know for sure if they will happen again. The only thing he can handle is a risk, which proves the importance of money management.

Vary The Size Of Its Positions?

Some traders use the same size regardless of the market configuration. They consider equiprobable events and believe that each configuration must, therefore, be assigned the same risk capital. This approach does not seem optimal for us and we think that it is necessary to vary the size of the position according to the opportunity that presents itself: to increase the size of its position when the opportunity seems excellent and its potential still important; reduce the size of the opportunity does not really give satisfaction, or even completely out of it.

It should be noted that novice traders do the opposite: at the outset, they allocate the same risk to all opportunities (good or bad); after a series of gains or losses, they increase the size of the position, whatever the opportunity, and take significant risks. They are suffering new losses that push them to engage more and more transactions, but also to increase the size of their positions, which can sometimes lead to ruin.

The performance relies heavily on the trader's ability to vary the size of his exposure based on opportunities. Likewise, it involves taking bigger risks and accepting higher drawdowns. Despite this, we remain convinced that good traders take much less risk than others and remain cautious in their decisions, even if they are not afraid to take positions. They consider that without risk-taking there are no possible gains.

This point of view was also defended by Thorp in his famous book Beat the dealer, which discusses the importance of increasing one's risk when probabilities are in our favor. Nevertheless, he also insists that conditions only favor 10% of the time and that it is during this period that we must maximize our chances of success. The payoff ratio must be favored over the probability of success.

Many traders place a lot of importance on the probability of success because it means that they are often more right than wrong. In fact, the payoff ratio has much more weight than the probability of success.

The payoff ratio is often low for traders

because of the psychological bias highlighted by Kahneman and Tversky. In fact, individuals have a much greater aversion for losses than the satisfaction gained from the gains made: a loss is twice as painful as the satisfaction gained from a gain of the same amount. It is for this reason that people tend to take profits very quickly and not take their losses (so not to execute their stops) or even to ignore any information about them because they seem too painful.

Chapter 7. Options Definition and Function

Apart from the popular financial instruments available on the market today such as stocks and bonds, there are other instruments known as derivatives.

A derivative refers to a financial instrument that gets its value from other instruments or assets. One example of these derivatives would be options.

By definition, options are financial instruments derived from an underlying asset such as stocks or bonds. They present you with an opportunity to purchase an underlying security at a specific date and price. In other words, options represent contracts that allow you to buy and sell a certain value of an underlying asset at a particular price. Each contract specifies certain terms about the trade.

How Do They Work?

Options provide you with a very reliable way of investing in stock trading. Just like any other financial transaction, an options agreement or contract is made up of two people—a buyer and a seller.

An individual contract represents a number of shares of the underlying security. In most cases, one contract covers 100 shares of stock. The buyer always pays a certain amount against each contract as the premium fee. This amount is always determined by the type of underlying asset as well as the option strike price.

Traders often use options as a form of investment because of the limited number of risks involved in these derivatives. This is because options enable people to protect their real stocks from financial market exposure. However, care must be taken when dealing with options since, like anyother trade, it is very easy to lose a large amount of stock within a fraction of time. They involve high profits, but may also result in high risks if not handled well. Despite this, many people consider options as one of the best and most reliable financial instruments on the stock market.

Options as Derivatives

As stated earlier, options are not real stock. They are derivatives whose price is determined by the price of the underlying security. Other examples of derivatives include futures, swaps, forwards, calls, and puts among several others.

Since options only represent a certain asset, the contract entered by a buyer and seller only offers you the ability to trade on the options market. An option call gives you the right to purchase an underlying security at a specific cost and time whereas a put option grants you the capability to sell on the market at a specified period of time and cost.

Each option transaction represents two sides—the buying side and the selling side.

Selling of an option is also known as writing an

option. Each side of an option transaction involves its own rewards and risks. When a person buys an option, it is said that they have obtained a long position; when they sell an option, they have a short position. This applies to both call and put transactions.

In options trading, asset owners do not get involved in the transaction. Cash is only exchanged between the parties involved in the options transactions. Most of these transactions happen between investors, brokers, and market makers.

Chapter 8. Types of Options

Options come in two major types—put options and call options. Traders choose the kind of option to trade-in depending on whether they want to buy or sell on the options market.

Call Options

The call option options make it possible for you to purchase an underlying asset associated with the option in question. When a call option is in the money, the bid or strike price is less in value than the underlying stockprice. Traders always buy a call option when there is a possibility of its stock price to increase beyond the current bid price before the expiration is obtained. When this happens, the trader derives some profit from the call transaction.

Individuals who purchase call options are always known as holders. Once they acquire the option, they can sell it any time before the expiration date. The profit of any option is obtained by subtracting the strike price, premium, and transaction fees from the stock price. The resulting amount iswhat is called the intrinsic value. This difference is always a negative value when the trader has made a loss and zero value when no profit or loss has been realized.

The maximum amount that a trader can lose from an option is equivalent to its premium. This explains why most people purchase options and not the underlying security.

The call option comprises three components—the strike price, the premium, and the exercise or expiration date. The premium is the amount of money that a trader pays when acquiring a particular option. For instance, a trader may purchase a call

option with $55 as the strike price, a $5 premium, and an expiration period of one month; it means that you will pay the seller $5 as the premium. If the expiration date is reached before you exercise the option, you will only pay the $5. If let's say, a week later the price goes up to $70 and you decide to sell your option, you will make a profit of $15 from the transaction less $5 paid as the premium. If the price goes below
$55, you make a loss.

Investors may also decide to sell a call option when they are anticipating a decline in the stock price. As the stock price falls to a level that is lowerthan the strike price, the investor will get some profit from the transaction. The person selling a call is known as the writer of the call. They must sell shares to a buyer at a price determined beforehand.

Put Options

This grants you the ability to write or sell an asset or security at a cost thatis already predetermined, also the expiration date. Both call and put options can be used on stocks, commodities, currencies, and indexes as underlying securities. In this case, the strike price becomes the cost by which you sell the option.

A put option allows you to sell a certain asset at a known cost and expiration date. This option can be used on a good number of underlying assets including indexes, currencies, commodities, and stocks. The price at which a trader sells an option is called the strike price.

Traders make a profit from selling a put option when anticipating a decline in the strike price. They make a loss when the value of the stock increasesto a level that is beyond the strike price. This indicates that the cost of a put option may rise or fall as time elapses.

The intrinsic value of a put option can be derived by obtaining the difference in the prices of the stock and the option. The resultant valuekeeps changing as the time value reduces in strength. When a stock option bears a positive intrinsic value, you say that it is in the money. A negative value of this shows that the option has fallen out of the money.

Similar to call options, you do not need to wait for your put options toexpire before you exercise them. Since the premium value of an option continues to vary with the price of the shares or the cost of any other underlying asset, you must exercise your options just at the right time to avoid incurring losses in the future.

Options and Stocks

If you have been keen enough then you must have realized that more investors are joining the options market more than the stock market. Stock trading has for a long time been the most popular form of trading on financial markets. You may be wondering if indeed options trading is better than stock trading. One great aspect of options is that they allow you to do more than just trading. Options have several characteristics that cannot be found in other financial instruments. One such characteristic is the use of Greeks, which are mathematical figures that help estimate the risk associated with each option. Traders can use these figures to avoid some trades that seem too risky.

There are several other differences between options

and stocks. When you purchase shares of stock from a certain company, you acquire ownership of the percentage of the company. This means that you can sell off the shares anytime you wish to do so.

On the other hand, options do not grant you ownership of stocks. They only represent derivatives of the company stocks that are traded on certain predefined terms.

The main reason why investors purchase stocks is to sell them later when the price goes high. They, therefore, wait for the value of a certain stock to decline before making a purchase, then again wait for the price to go up in order to sell the same. When it comes to options, investors use them as a way of generating income and not necessarily as a form of investment. Options traders are never interested in the underlying stock. Most of them trade on short-term engagements. This is why the options market is always filled with almost all kinds of traders.

The trader relies on certain changes in the performance of the option to make money.

Another clear difference between stocks and options is the issue of time. Stocks can be traded for as long as decades. They do not have an expiration period.

Once you invest in the stock market, it may take you as little as a few days to as much as several years to close your positions and make a profit. However, this can only happen when the company issuing the shares continues to exist. This privilege is missing in the options market since each option has a specific date of expiration.

Most people who invest in stocks always end up with good profits in the long-term. This is because most companies that sell shares keep building their brand portfolio, making it impossible for them to collapse. As the company grows, the share value grows as well. When it comes to options, the value a trader receives at the end of each transaction is very uncertain. Options trading is somehow likened to gambling, which may end in a winor loss.

Each trade involves a number of aspects that determine the outcome. It is upon the trader to understand these aspects and apply them accurately in order to realize a profit. Ignoring the rules of trade always results in a loss.

Another great difference between stocks and options is that stocks arealways sold in the form of preferred stocks or common stocks while optionsare traded in the form of contracts. Common stocks are those that cover a percentage of the participation in the profit of the company while preferred stocks are those that pay dividends to the investor. Traders receive these dividends at predefined intervals and amounts. Options contracts, on the other hand, serve as agreements between the buyer and the seller based on certain terms that both have to agree upon.

The pricing of stocks and options also differs.

The value of each stock share depends on how the company performs in the long-run, as well as some market factors. On the other hand, the cost of options is determined by an array of factors such as time decay, expiration date as well as the value of the underlying security.

In terms of risk, a stock trader only risks losing their capital if the company underperforms or stops operating. This means that if the company continues to operate, the trader is sure of getting most of their capital back with some profit. In options, the highest value that a trader can lose is equivalent to the amount of capital invested in each position. Since there is an unlimited potential of losing the premium, it means that options trading involves more risk than stock trading. It may take years for a stock investor to lose part of their capital; however, it takes a matter of minutes or hours for an options trader to lose their premium.

Chapter 9. The Options Contract

An options contract is an agreement providing you with the authority or right to acquire or give out an asset for a specific amount of money. Basically, an options contract represents 100 shares of stock.

Each contract is defined by two categories of people—buyers and sellers. To purchase or sell options, the involved parties must fulfill the rules or formalities stipulated in the contract. In some cases, cash is used to settle contracts instead of shares.

For every contract, the person buying or acquiring a purchase position is the holder, and the seller is known as the writer. An option that is not exercised during the stipulated timeframe expires at the end of this period. One good thing with options is that the loss is often deducted from the money you put in as capital. Once an option expires, you can no longer engage in transactions based on the underlying stock.

The payoff pattern for stocks is almost similar to the one used in stock trading. The contract acts as a form of leverage for each transaction. This is because the holder or writer of each contract only gets control of a small percentage of the underlying security.

This means that traders only get the rights to a tiny portion relating to the stock being traded.

During each transaction, businesspeople can keep reinvesting their profits into the same position until the option expires. This gives the trader good leverage during price fluctuations. It is always easy for a trader to exercise an option before its value starts to diminish. This is one way of minimizing the risk of losing all the premium invested in the market. Options contract provide several details about the market and the trade. Justlike any other trade, you are required to make some payment before you tart trading. Each contract is governed by a number of terms definedbelow:

Derivative

We have defined options as forms of other instruments. This is a contract between traders with a value that is dictated by the value of underlying security. For each contract that involves derivatives, involved parties must first agree on the initial cost of the underlying asset. Options are considered derivatives since they only give you the right over a percentage of certain commodities.

Strike Price

This describes the cost or value of an option at any particular time. The strike price can also be referred to as the agreed-upon price. It is the cost of an option agreed upon by the buyer and the seller when making an options contract.

In the case of a call option, the strike price is the value placed as the cost a trader pays to gain rights around the underlying stock. In terms of the put option, the strike price generally implies the cost about which the seller relinquishes the rights to security.

This price does not change during the period of

the contract. It is not affected by any market and stock elements. Strike prices are some of the determinants of the profit one can make from the market. If underlying stock prices rise beyond the amount of the strike price, one of the things that will rise is the cost of the option and this is the best time for sellers to close their positions at a profit. When the value of the stock drops below the strike price, buyers can purchase options at this point with the hope that the same price will rise. When there is a variation in regards to the strike price and with relations to the price of the market, this variation is what will be used to calculate the profit.

Expiration

What expiration means is a period when a given options get to an end. When the exercise date is attained, it means that it is no longer available for trading. The difference between the start and end dates of an option is known as its time period.

The value of an option often decreases as it approaches the expiration date. In most cases, this date can range from a few hours, days, or even years.

The Underlying Security

This is the asset used to define an options contract. It is the underlying stock upon which you trade your options. It is an essential component of the options market since it enables you to come up with the price and risks associated with certain stocks. It also allows you to choose the right options with the highest profit potential. In most cases, the cost of any option is determined using the worth of the underlying security.

Share

Shares are units of stock belonging to a certain company. Each option represents 100 shares of stock.

Contract Size

The contract size is the number of shares or stocks represented by a given option contract.
For example, if a contract covers 100 shares, then

100 is the contract size.

The Premium

We have mentioned this severally before. The premium is the price you need to pay in order to acquire rights on an option. The premium can also be defined as the income that you receive from selling or writing an options contract. It can also refer to the cost of a given contract before it expires. In most cases, the premium is quoted in terms of dollars per share. The premium highlights a combination of three components—the time component, intrinsic component, and implied volatility of the asset.

Traders obtain the intrinsic value from calculations based on subtracting the asset cost from the strike cost. In a call option, this amount is equivalent to the current cost of the stock or security less the strike price. In the case of a put option, this value equals the amount set as the strike price minus the cost of the current stock.

When it comes to the options trading business, what is known as the time value comprises the amount a trader is willing to pay, with the hope that market prices will change in their favor. This time value drops when the option approaches the exercise date. Basically, how much more time is available before the expiration of an option, the higher its time value. Whenmore time is available, it is easy for investors to pay more premium for the option with the hope that its price will change in the future. When there is less time until the expiration of an option, more traders will shy away from investing in the option since very little price change is expected.

The premium, therefore, is an addition between the option time value and the intrinsic value of the option.

Chapter 10. Options Trading

Most people always think of the stock market when they want to invest. Actually, a good number of stock market traders do not understand what options trading is all about. Stock trading has several benefits; however, it may not work for individuals who wish to invest on a short-term basis. Long-term investment strategies such as the buy and hold can help investors increase their wealth significantly, however such strategies do not provide better profits like some short-term ones. This is where more active short-term methods like options trading come in. These are often characterized by more returns.

Options trading has continued to become more and more popular. Basically, it involves the trading of financial derivatives known as options. The concept of options trading is not new. The first options contract was made in 1973 at an Exchange in the Chicago Board. There is a lot of similarity between the options traded today and those used at that time. However, a lot of things have changed in terms of the market size, trading terms, and the volume of exchange carried out every single day. People invest in options for various reasons, which will be discussed later in this chapter.

Options trading is a great way of investing money. Both the wealthy and average people can invest in the business since it does not require a lot of capital to start. Like we mentioned earlier, options are contracts that work within specific time limits.

Trading styles for options do differ from one region to another. This means that options can be categorized as American, European, Barrier,

Bermudan, or Exotic options among several others. When trading options, you must be able to tell the style involved to enjoy the necessary gains. American options, for instance, close at the end of every third Friday of the month of expiry. The price of an option on this date becomes the closing price for the position. One major characteristic of American options is that you can close any moment between start and exercise days. European options, on the other hand, must be exercised on the date of expiration and not before. Positions for these options close on the third Thursday of the expiration month. There are also barrier options, which can only be exercised after the stock value rises beyond a certain level.

Bermudan ones are to be closed anywhere between start and exercise dates while exotic options make use of non-standard exercise procedures.

What Is Involved in Options Trading?

Basically, options trading involves the buying and selling of options contracts in the options market. Traders make a profit by purchasing contracts at relatively low costs and selling the same at higher costs.

When you buy a call option, it is like you are betting that the share price will rise in the future. For instance, if you purchase a call option for company X for $1500, you are indicating your certainty that the cost of the asset will shoot upwards beyond this purchase price for you to make a profit. Every time you purchase a put option, you are anticipating a decline in the cost of the underlying security. In stock market terms, you are expecting a bearish outcome on the stock.

Options trading is more flexible than stock trading. This is because options are derived from a wide array of underlying securities. This gives traders more variety in terms of the scope involved in the trade. Investors use the price of options to determine price movements of stocks, commodities, foreign currencies, and indices.

This presents a lot of profit-making opportunities that may not be present in the stock market. More versatility is also realized in the numerous types of options and orders that traders can place on the market.

Stock traders only have two ways through which they can make a profit— that is long positions and short positions. However, in options trading, investors get spoilt for choice since positions can be executed in several diverse ways and combinations.

Purchasing Options

Purchasing an options contract is just similar to purchasing stock. Investors buy options by selecting what they wish to buy, stating the amount then placing a buy to open order either directly or indirectly through a broker. If he value of the option goes up, you can sell it or exercise it depending on what works for you. One serious advantage of options trading is that you can make money from price increases and also from price declines. If you anticipate a rise in the prices, you can buy a call option and if you anticipate a drop in the prices, you can purchase a put option.

When you decide to buy an option, you will get several contracts on the same underlying stock. This will be in terms of the types of calls and puts available for the same stock. For instance, you may find an option for company selling at $100 for each share, and find several others for the same company selling at different premiums.

Buying a Call Option

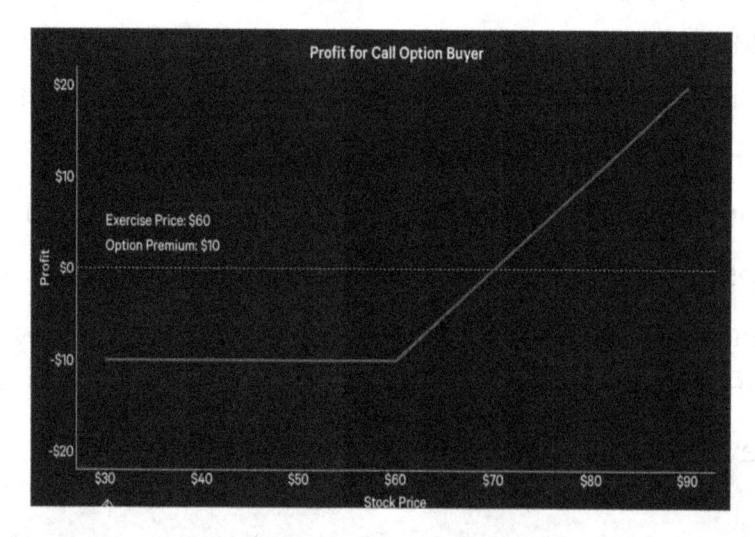

Let us assume that you want to purchase a call option for company A with an exercise cost of $60, a premium of $10, and an expiration date of one month. 7 days later, the stock price increases to $75. This means that you will make some $15 from the transaction. However, since you had already paid a premium of $10 to place the order, your profit will be $15 less $10 which comes to $5.

This is as illustrated below.

Figure 1: Buying a Call

If the price of stock declines to, say, $50 per share and you decide to let the option expire on its own. You will get an outlay of -$10, which is equivalentto the premium you paid for the order.

Buying a Put Option

Let us also assume that you are purchasing a put option from company Afor $45, a premium rate of $15, and an expiration of one month. After one week, the price drops from $45 to $25. If you exercise the option at this point, you will get a difference of $20. Your profit at their point will be $20 less than the premium that is $5.

Selling Options

Writing or selling of contracts occurs in two ways. The first one is whenyou have pre-bought contracts that you want to release at a profit; similarly, in a position when you do not want to suffer more losses, then you can place a sell to close order on the options market. You can raise this order if the price of the option has gone up and you want to get some profit from this change, or if the option price is constantly falling and you want to close the position before you incur more losses.

The second way is through opening short positions. This is what is known as the writing of options because the strategy involves creating new contracts for the options market. When a buyer agrees to your contract, you will be obliged to sell the underlying security associated with the contract to them.

The process of writing options is often completed using the sell to open order. The seller receives a payment that is equivalent to the strike price as soon as they place this order. Using such orders may sometimes be riskier than engaging in ordinary buying and selling, but it may also come with higher returns in terms of profit. Most investors place the sell-to-open order when they are certain that the buyer will not close a contract early enough as they seek to generate some income.

Selling Calls

This involves allowing the buyer to make purchases against an asset or underlying equity. The market prices and other factors may force a seller to give away some equity with the price agreed on earlier as the strike price.

When the investor selling a call option also turns out to be the one owning the underlying equity, the process gets the name "writing a covered call." If the person selling the same option turns out not to be the one owning the stock, then the process gets referred to as "writing a naked call."

Selling a Put Option

Besides buying put options, you may also sell them at a profit. Investors who sell put options do so with the hope that the options will lose value in the future. When a trader sells a put option to the buyer, they have some authority to acquire the equity involved in the trade at a predefined cost if the option is exercised. For the seller to make a profit, the cost of the equity should remain either as it is or goes higher beyond the current strike cost. In case the cost remains under the strike cost, the involved seller makes a loss while the buyer makes a profit from the trade.

When it comes to options trading, profit is made from selling, buying, and writing options, not necessarily by exercising them. The point at which a trader exercises a contract depends on the strategies used in the trade aswell as the need to acquire underlying security. This means that you can make a profit both from exercising options and from just buying and sellingthem.

Expiration

One aspect that governs options is their expiration capability. At the end of each expiration period, the trader realizes a profit or loss. The reason why most traders try to learn and apply as many strategies as possible to each trade is that they want to realize profits for each contract. Most traders always feel frustrated when a contract ends without yielding any profit.

The profit of an option is determined by its intrinsic

as well as time value. This is why it is important to consider the expiration period of any contract before investing in it. Some options may seem promising in terms of profitsbut end up at a loss because of the short expiration period. Options also do exist only for the period of time that the underlying stock is available on themarket for trading. Once a company stops listing its stock on the market,the options related to this particular stock will cease to trade as well.

The more an investor holds onto options, the more its value decreases. Unlike stocks, options tend to expire faster, and as the expiration date nears,the possibility of making profits from the trade also diminishes. Professional traders always ensure that they get more out of an open contract before it gets too late.

Chapter 11. The Volatility of the Options Market

In the options market, the term volatility describes the way the cost of a specific equity fluctuates over a period of time. Highly volatile options are often derived from highly volatile stocks; these carry more risks. Options with low volatility are always a featureless risk. In the options market, those stocks that feature high volatility always cost more than those with low volatility. It is not easy to identify certain stocks in terms of their volatility levels since it is easier for some low volatility stocks to become highly volatile and vice versa. Volatility is of two types—implied or historic.

The historical type of volatility is alternatively called statistical volatility. It measures price fluctuations based on predetermined time frames. It helps you to determine how the price of a particular option fluctuates over a period of time, say one year. A rise in historical volatility increases the cost of the equity in question. When this amount drops, the price of equity also goes back to normal. By understanding the changes in options prices over time, investors can make informed decisions on when and how to invest in a particular type of option. For instance, if the historical volatility of a particular option for 6 months is 25% and the volatility over the last 5 days is 50% it means that the stock has a volatility that is higher than normal.

Implied volatility, on the other hand, refers to the estimation of a particular stock or future volatility of the option based on some market factors. It is also known as projected volatility and is mostly used by traders who wantto determine the future prices of certain options. This type of volatility is often derived from the cost of a given option. Traders make use of the price as well as the historical performance of an option to determine its future price trends.

In case you are purchasing an option that has a high potential to generate profit, the premium of such an option may be higher than other options. This is because you can easily sell the option at a profit. Such positions are claimed to be in the money. Another trade may be "at the money" indicatingthat the cost is similar to the price of the equity.

There is another one that can get "out of the money," which means that the cost of trading the option is way higher than the value of the equity. An option like this one is not good since it is almost impossible for you to get some profit from it.

Once a call option gets in the money, it indicates that the cost of the equity has shot higher than the strike cost. When a put option gets in the money, the cost of the underlying equity is far below the strike cost.

If there is still a wide time gap between the beginning and end of a trade transaction, more time is available for a trader to make a profit.

Chapter 12. Benefits of Options Trading

One major reason why people invest in options is the level of risk involved and the returns realized. By now, you must have noticed the huge difference between trading with options and trading directly with stocks. Options can be traded in combination with other financial instruments to leverage profits. The trade is easily carried out and, in most cases, the profits arevery good.

Options are considered by many people as a great alternative to stocktrading. They do not cost much and help secure your underlying assets during the trade. Let us look at some of the major advantages that options have over other investment tools.

Options Involve Lower Costs

We have already mentioned the fact that options have a high potential for generating large profits for small capital investments. Most people trade-in options as an alternative to other forms of investment for this particular reason. Even those with very little capital can gain significant profit from the trade so long as they apply the right knowledge and strategies.

This means that traders can open an option position with the same potential as a stock position using lower amounts of capital. Let us say for example, that you wish to purchase 100 shares of stock at $80 for each share. This means that you will need to raise $8000 to make this purchase. However, if you were to buy the same shares using two call options, each with apremium of $20, then you will need half of the total capital for the same value of the stock. This is because each call represents 100 shares. Twocalls will represent 200 shares, multiplying this by $20 per share comes to $4000.

The low costs of trading options are quite

advantageous because they give investors the potential to raise large amounts of income over a short period of time. This advantage is absent in a number of financial instruments, especially those that are long-term since large amounts of cash must be invested in such instruments to generate income.

Options Are Associated with Reduced Risk Levels

Each financial investment tool bears a number of risks and this also applies to options trading. For most of these tools, it is always assumed that the higher the risk, the higher the returns. However, this is not true with optionssince there is a high balance between the risk and reward of each transaction. On most occasions, the risk of a trade is very little compared to the reward realized. Some market factors make it possible for traders to make a profit at very low risks. One great advantage of the options marketis that you get to choose the kind of strategy you want to use in your transactions by first determining the amount of risk you are willing to expose your investment. You can always balance various strategies and market factors to balance or lower the risk involved in each position. The more you understand the basics of options trading, the more you will know how to minimize the risks involved in the trade.

The success of each trade always depends on the trader's ability to mitigate risks. If you do not understand how to measure risks and work around them, it may be difficult for you to generate profit from some transactions. Although there is still a high risk of losing your capital when trading options, this risk is relatively low compared to the risk of trading stocks or underlying securities. The only amount you may lose from trading options is the premium amount. If you analyze your contracts correctly and stick to the rules of trade all the way, you will always make some profit from options trading.

The strategies used in assessing options help investors to calculate the risk involved in certain contracts before putting their money in any of these contracts. This makes it easy for traders to estimate the expected profits and losses in good time. With such information, you can easily delve into the trade with confidence knowing what you should expect from the market. By using the right trading styles and sticking to the right strategies, you can easily reduce losses and make the most out of each trading period. In a nutshell, it is in order to say that options feature limited risks and unlimited profits.

When the cost of an option has not favored you by the time of expiration, you can allow it to expire worthlessly, but you will lose your premium. This is why, just like any other form of investment, it is advisable that you only invest what you can afford to lose. The level of risk involved depends on your level of expertise and commitment. If you become careless in your trades, the risks may increase and you may end up losing each time.

Chapter 13. Options Help You to Generate Passive Income

The options market involves the use of several strategies. Some of these strategies can help you generate some passive income from the trade. For instance, the covered call strategy allows you to purchase stock, then earn some cash selling calls from the same stock to investors. This way, you are still the owner of the stock, but making some returns from the stock at the same time.

Other strategies assist you in making maximum use of market factors such as volatility and time decay. Options spread and combination strategies alsoassist you in gaining more from the market. As you trade, you may keep growing your stock from the returns.

If you add more shares to a stock that pays dividends, you will be able to grow your income significantly.

Chapter 14. Options Provide Leverage for Your Investment

For each option contract that you start, you either purchase or sell 100shares of stock. This means that you can gain control over a large numberof shares without utilizing large amounts of capital.

This is because the amount you need to trade an option is far much less than the exact price of the shares.

By spending less on each contract, you will be able to enter more positions and trade in large amounts of underlying stocks within a shorter period of time. As a result, you will multiply your profits faster and this will translate faster growth of your investments.

Buying an options contract does not give you any right to the underlying shares. You only gain access to a small percentage of the underlying security.

If the other party decides to exercise the contract before expiration, there is very little and, in some cases, nothing to lose. Since the value of an option is affected by several other factors besides the value of the underlying asset, it is very easy to make good money from positions even atthe time that the cost of the underlying equity has not made any significant change. This explains the reason why the options market has both small as well as more established investors.

Options Offer More Flexibility and Versatility

Options trading is very flexible. This is one of the many factors that make investors flood the options market. The contracts always feature the most versatile terms and the strategies involved in the trade are quite diverse. Traders can comfortably apply a combination of strategies on a singlecontract to make the best in terms of capital.

Options are also bought and sold depending on a wide array of underlying assets.

asides understanding the direction, which prices may take, you can alsoget to find out how the prices of foreign currencies, indices, and commodities can change in the future. This helps you to know the type of underlying security you need to go for to ensure that you get quick profits.

With the many strategies in place, it becomes very easy to determine the kind of opportunities to invest in. For instance, if you are skilled in determining changes in the foreign exchange market, you can easily apply this skill in the options market to determine how the market is going to change over time. One great strategy that ensures flexibility of options trading is the use of spreads. You can significantly reduce the cost of trading by incorporating certain spreads and combinations. These not only reduce the risk of entering certain positions but also enable you to make a profit from price changes in more than one direction. In uncertain trades, you can use these strategies to hedge certain positions as a way of minimizing losses.

You may also use options to create synthetic trade positions, which offer you several opportunities that help you to attain your profit goals. These positions are commonly used by experts and provide a great alternative to the normal strategies used in options trading.

Flexibility in options trading is also enhanced by how people use their time. When it comes to options, it is not a must for you to spend all day watching the market for you to gain profit. Options allow you to create your contracts based on predicted price movements. This is totally different from the buy and holds strategies used in other investment tools. If you invest in an option contract with a high probability of success, it is not a must that you spend time monitoring the trade. You can define stop-loss orders to ensure that a contract position closes as soon as the direction of the market changes.

Besides all this, you also have the opportunity to dictate the duration of each contract. You can, therefore, trade on a daily, weekly, monthly, or even annual basis depending on the amount of time you have. For instance, if you have more time within the day, you can take up daily positions.

The benefits listed above explain why options trading has been appealing to a good number of investors. The process is quite simple and a lot of profit can be made within a short time period. When you balance your contracts properly, you can easily reduce risks in your overall portfolio. For example, you may decide to combine selling stock and buying a put option at the same time. This will grant you an advantage when the stock price goes up, and limit losses in case of the stock price decreases. When coming up with a trading plan for the options market, you must beware of every aspect involved in the market. First, you must understand what account you need to be able to trade, as well as the amount of capital required as premium. With a good plan, you will be able to trade successfully and keep improving with time.

Conclusion

Hone your intuition: If you hope to be a successful day trader then you are going to need to get into the habit of making popular trades before they become popular for the best results. As such, you need to get into the habit of always following the beat of your own drum when it comes to drawing conclusions from your research and acting accordingly. While this doesn't mean listening to your gut, if you have put in the time and done the work and it all points in a direction that no one else has gone in yet then you need to be confident enough in your abilities to get in before things turn in that direction and you miss out on profits that were by all rights yours to lose. Knowing when to separate yourself from the pack is what separates average day traders from rich ones.

While this sounds relatively straightforward in theory, in practice, it is much more often about understanding when a certain trade is being hyped by those with something to gain and when the facts are actually pointing in a specific direction. While the most surefire way to learn the difference is through experience, eventually you will be able to determine the difference between a good trade and a good story and make money off the sheep who aren't aware there is a difference in the process. If you are having trouble believing in yourself in this way, then the best way to bolster your confidence is to start with listening to your intuition on smaller trades.

The success of any type will make it easier to trust yourself on more important trades in the future and should be celebrated appropriately to ensure they will be remembered the next time a similar situation arises. Remember, just because you are trading in short time frames doesn't mean you need to rush the decisions you make, only by fully thinking through every decision that you make will you know that you have truly made the right decision. A rash decision is a surefire way to lose money, no two ways around it.

Never let your losses build: As a new trader, it can be easy to become emotionally invested in the stocks you choose which is why it is crucial that you learn to separate your expectations for a trade from the reality of what occurs when the rubber meets the road. To successfully ensure that you don't lose more than the bare minimum on a given trade it is important that you cut its lose the second it stops generating a profit as opposed to hanging on to it in hopes that it turns around and rebounds in the correct direction.

It is important to learn early that a failed trade is not a reflection on you as a trader but simply a part of the natural trading process. Sticking with a losing trade is rarely, if ever, going to result in that trade turning around, and if it does the results are going to be middling at best. Likewise, it is never a good idea to double down on a losing trade as a means of mitigating a potential loss. Adding to a losing position is akin to trying to dig yourself out of a hole, it is never going to work no matter how hard you want it to.

Understand that sometimes the market simply has nothing to offer when many new traders get into the habit of buying up stocks, they feel as though they need to keep it up, even if the market isn't presenting anything worthwhile at the moment. It is important to understand that quality is going to supersede quantity every single time. Making changes to the stocks you are holding too often can easily decrease your profit margins and hurt your trading plan in the process as it will be difficult to determine just how effective you are actually being. Rather, it is always a better choice to simply let your current investments matriculate and wait until something that is actually better comes along before you do anything rash. Extra trades mean extra chances for loss, while poorly researched trades mean extra chances for loss as well. With these types of odds is it any wonder why these types of trades can quickly destroy all your profits?

Focus on yourself: If you are looking for a way to lose money while day trading, there will never be a more effective means of doing so than by trying to follow the trading plans that work for other people. A trading plan is an extremely personal expression of your goals for the market of your choice and the way that you are going to interact with it. As such, it requires plenty of trial and error, as well as personal introspection to ensure that it works with your natural trading tendencies as opposed to against them.

While looking at the level of success that professional traders have can make it difficult to forge your own path, mimicking what they are trying to do is only going to prove to be an exercise in futility ultimately. It is important to instead avoid the temptation by keeping in mind that knowing yourself and your strengths and weaknesses is the most reliable path to success.

Avoid trades that are out of the money: While there are a few strategies out there that make it a point of picking up options that are currently out of the money, you can rest assured that they are most certainly the exception, not the rule. Remember, the options market is not like the traditional stock market which means that even if you are trading options based on underlying stocks buying low and selling high is just not a viable strategy. If a call has dropped out of the money, there is generally less than a 10 percent chance that it will return to acceptable levels before it expires which means that if you purchase these types of options what you are doing is little better than gambling, and you can find ways to gamble with odds in your favor of much higher than 10 percent.

Always consider the source of tips: As a new day trader, you will likely be on the lookout for potential trading advice from anywhere and everywhere you can find it. This is a perfectly natural response to the magnitude of possible opportunities out there, and it can even be fruitful in the long run, but only if you know whose tips you should trust and whose you should take with a grain of salt. Many dubious tips start off from an honest place, someone you know who is talking about a company that is soon going to do something like releasing a new killer product, have groundbreaking earnings or who is going to be purchased by a major conglomerate.

Additionally, you will find many financial personalities on television touting this type of asset or that as the be all and end all of trading. While occasionally these types of tips will pay out, in general, the financial personality will have a stake in the investment, or it will turn out to just be the new fad for the next few months before it is forgotten entirely. This is not to say that you should avoid all trading tips entirely, rather it is to point out that before you go ahead and make a move you are going to want to do your own research on the investment and then move forward only if you feel the reasoning behind the investment is sound.

Your notes